RIGHT ON TIME

TIME IS THE MOST POWERFUL TOOL THAT OFFERS YOU A CHANCE TO GET IT RIGHT.

by

TERESIA RAY WRIGHT

Table Of Content

Introduction

This book is written to impart hope that God will be right on time in any situation. There are moments of uncertainty in this world, and the enemy fights us as we travel through life. Whatever we encounter, never deviate from the plan of God because He has a miraculous plan to give us a beautiful future. Study His Word and trust Him to reveal His perfect plan for you. All God commands from His children is faith in Him as He guides us through life's uncertainties. The adversary attacks: but God will defend His children. He will not allow the adversary to rewrite His plan for our lives.

I vowed to God to pour my heart out in this book. My goal is to free someone from the enemy's deceptive spirit. He desires to keep you bound; when in actuality, you are free through God's son, Jesus Christ. You must remember that patience is the key because God always comes in His set time, and it is always right on time. When reading this book, may you experience God's love to a deeper degree and may your faith be elevated. I believe there will be some crying out to God and praises of thanksgiving. There may be occasional laughter at God's vast humor. Above all, may you gain boldness to speak with authority to the enemy when he attempts to use his deceptive devices against you and your family.

My hope is that after reading the entirety of this book, you will be more motivated to branch out into the world with a greater expectation of the magnitude of God's love and blessings that He has for you and your family. Stay focus; ask God to order your thoughts. No matter how the circumstances look, you are accountable for your own actions. Thoughts that are ordered by God do not dwell on evil. Ponder these inspired words in your heart. Use them to achieve total victory over every area in your life.

Dedication

To God, who has given me rivers of living water to drink from His Well of Inspiration.

To my deceased parents and siblings: whom I will see again in Paradise.

To the memory of my spiritual leaders, the late Bishop Ritchie and Pastor Lucille Ritchie who drew me to Christ at Freedom Life Ministries. I honor them for their unwavering love of God's people.

To my readers, if there be any doubt in your hearts may it be removed, and your faith in God be renewed.

Acknowledgements

I am extremely grateful for the love and support from so many people in my life during the writing of this book. Harold, my husband, thank you for your patience and love. I especially thank you for encouraging me to keep moving forward even when I wanted to quit. I love you unconditionally.

I extend a loving thanks to my three children: Vernita, William, Tanesha, and my grandchildren. Thank you for your help when I need it. I am honored to be your mother and grandmother.

Margaret and Michael, my only living siblings; you have always remained true to our parents' and aunt's wishes that we stay together in love and support. Thank you for loving and supporting me through this process.

My two sons-in-law: Terry, who is my pastor at Giving God the Praise Ministries, and Delaunta, who is my helper. Thank you for giving me one less thing to be concerned about by loving, protecting, and providing for my daughters and grandchildren.

Many thanks to my mother-in-law, Dorothy, who treats me as her daughter. Thank you for always sharing the inspirational Word of God with me.

Ruth, my niece, thank you for providing constructive feedback on my manuscript.

I thank my friend, Bobbie, for the tireless hours contributed to proofreading, revising, and collaborating during the writing of this book.

Thank you, God, for providing me with the amazing team to make this book possible!

ABOUT THE AUTHOR

Minister Topfavor is a native of Montgomery, Alabama. She has a Bachelor of Science degree in Sociology where she applies her sociological skills in helping people with various issues. She is a spirit-filled, ordained minister of the Gospel of Jesus Christ and committed to her local church. She and her family attend Giving God the Praise Ministries where Terrance Watkins serves as the pastor. She ministers the Word of God at her local church and surrounding churches within the city of Montgomery. Minister Topfavor believes that the Lord has called her to sound the alarm of urgency. Her goal is to inspire people to give their lives to Jesus and follow the plan for life that God has designed through His Holy Word. She believes that God inspires her to share the gospel of Jesus with heartfelt love that is void of judgment. Minister Topfavor holds numerous positions in the church. However, she feels that people need to be reminded and forewarned to live a life that is in alignment with God's Word. To this end, she hopes to continue her ministry of godly teaching, counseling, and writing for many years to come.

CHAPTER ONE
A Timeless God

As humans, we must acknowledge that God moves in His set time because He is a timeless God who is not bound by space and time. Although God is not bound by time, He promises His children that in due season, we shall reap a harvest. Every return received from God is always on time because He is perfect in everything, but humans are not. Humans interact with time on routine schedules, such as morning, noon, evening, and night. Humans also interact with time during seasonal changes: winter, fall, spring, and summer. As humans, we are subject to make mistakes in our daily interactions with time.

Praying to my heavenly Father helps me throughout the day, which gives me a sense of peace that I am covered by the blood of Jesus. I am not a morning person, but the first thing I do when I awake is open my eyes, just smile, remember that life is good, and thank the Lord for another day. Then, I bow down and pray to my heavenly father in the name of Jesus for myself, my family, my friends, and others. I thank Him that I did not get a phone call in the middle of the night informing me that something tragic had happened to my family.

Even when we pray for others, God honors our prayers because the sincere prayers of the righteousness of God avails much. The righteousness of God is believers in Christ who are determined to live by faith and strive to please God on a daily basis. God has a plan for our lives that supersede our plans. There is nothing wrong with a plan, but we must remember God can and will alter our plans to give us a better future.

My mine goes back to when I was working in a t-shirt factory, and I said to the ladies, "I will work for this company only three years." My plan was totally different from God's plan. I worked an additional ten years, thirteen years sewing collars onto t-shirts. I prayed the sincere prayer of the righteousness of God, and when a believer prays intense prayer to God through His son Jesus Christ, the believer will always receive the victory. However, we have to wait on God's plan because, the majority of the time, our plans differ from God's plan.

Although I was still an employee at the t-shirt factory, I kept seeking better employment. God led me to college, but I had no desire to attend college. I wanted my money, and I wanted it now! Actually, I wanted to earn more money to provide a better life for my three children and myself. In my heart, I knew God was leading me in the right direction, but it appeared to be a long process.

I attended a technical college to receive training in computer clerical skills. To make a long story short, I attended college and worked part-time clerical jobs for approximately two years. During this time, I applied for several positions, including a bank position. For months, I did not have any resources. In addition to that, my mother's second oldest daughter passed. I was out-of-town attending my sister's funeral when I received a call from the bank that I was chosen for the position and was informed that the orientation class began at eight o'clock Monday morning. On Sunday we departed from the out-of-town trip and arrived home after driving sixteen hours. We arrived home at 7:00 A.M. I had thirty minutes to shower, dress, and drive to the orientation.

During this status of unemployment, God tested my faith to observe if I would trust Him or turn to other sources to meet my needs. I must say it was not easy, but it was worth waiting for because it worked in my favor. I received the position and advanced speedily to a higher position in the company. I remember what the elders always said: "God may not come when you want Him, baby, but He is always on time." That is one of the truest statements ever. I bear witness to that statement today and forever.

We must acknowledge that God's thoughts are not our thoughts, and His ways are not our ways. His Word is forever settled in heaven; therefore, we must wait patiently for Him to answer our prayers. Sometimes it is difficult to wait patiently when you have a lack of food and clothing, your utility bills are thirty days due, and an eviction notice on your home. However, you must remember that Jesus did it before, and He will do it again.

During my dry season, I endeavor to energize my faith because God never does anything accidentally; everything He does has a purpose. I did not understand why my life was moving in a spiral direction. However, in my darkest moments, I always observed a shining light piercing through the tunnel. I learned early in life that in our waiting season, we have much to learn in our walk with the Lord, more to change in our daily relationships, and surely more to grow in areas where we are weak. However, the only thing that will give a Christian comfort when he or she is burdened is prayer, praise, and the Word of God.

If the unsaved is burdened, to lift that burden is to accept Jesus Christ as the savior and embrace God's power in their lives. A friend of mine asked her brother if she could pray for him to accept Jesus and let Jesus make him whole because the doctors were not hopeful of any recovery for this man. However, the brother advised his sister that he did not want any part of her God. This man died without a savior. Of course, we have a right to choose our own destiny. Without our right to choose, then judgment would not be a necessity. God gives us the power of choice; therefore, judgment will be whether we accept Jesus or not. That is why some will be saved, and some will die without a savior. I urge you to not miss your chance for salvation and die without a savior. Time is of the essence because we do not know our expiration date in life; only God knows our beginning and end.

On another note, countless people are captivated by their own actions because many think that they are untouchable. But God can, and He will knock you right off of your high horse.

The bible gives a prime example of this: the Word of God recorded that a man had an encounter with Jesus on the road to Damascus. His name was Saul, but later changed to Paul. Before the transition, Saul was traveling from city to city, going into people's homes and taking Christians to jail. Jesus knocked him off his horse and blinded him. Sometimes we think when a person acts uncommonly for such a long time, that nothing is going to change. We are accountable for our good and bad choices on the earth, just like Saul. Saul arrested God's people, and I believe those Christians were praying that the Lord would come to their rescue, and He did. Jesus revealed Himself as God and put Saul in check. God is doing the same thing today to those that persecute His people. God chastised Saul for his aggressive treatment of His people. After Saul's encounter with Jesus, he became Paul and was one of the greatest apostles of Jesus.

Allow me to attempt to explain the difference between God's chastising and God's chastening. Chastising is punishment, some type of physical force. Chastising is what happened to Saul. Saul was blinded by a bright light. God stopped him from persecuting the church and converted him to Christianity. Chasten can be delicate and mild. God chastens those He loves, meaning He corrects those whom He loves. A child of God is not punished by God, but they can and will be chastened by Him. The more we recognize our dependence on God, the more thankful we become when He is chastening us. This will increase our love for Him and our reverence towards Him. God is love and our greatest continual need should be to better know and love Him. As Christians, we must use wisdom-especially when we are sharing the Word of God. There are two things that are a red flag to me in sharing the gospel. A believer who is ministering to a seeker becomes angry or uses scare tactics if the seeker chooses not to accept Jesus as his personal savior. God does not want us to become angry with people if they do not accept His love. Our commitment is to persuade nonbelievers according to the Word of God. If they are reluctant to accept Jesus as their personal savior, then the Christians' obligation is to pray that God will continue to give them the opportunity to make the most important decision of their lives. That decision is to accept His son, Jesus. As far as scare tactics, God gives us an opportunity to receive His son through His Word. He does not want Christians to force or use scare tactics to get someone to accept Jesus. There are people who send scare tactics messages on Facebook, Instagram, and other websites to force people to Christ. These are immature carnal minded Christians. Carnal minded Christians are those who live according to the flesh and set their minds on the things of the flesh. Bluntly, carnal minded people have resistance against God because they focus on glory for themselves. Scare tactics are an incorrect way to invite anyone into a life-giving relationship with Christ. Manipulating someone into becoming a Christian is absurd and void of free-will.

Jesus is only requesting that believers affirm the biblical truth. This walk with the Lord is not threatening and does not force an immediate, emotion-based decision onto a person. It is a choice that one makes upon hearing the truth, responding to the truth, and waiting on God to draw them to His son. If an individual does not accept Jesus as the savior, the Bible describes hell as real, and an individual will burn in the brimstone and fire. Nevertheless, we should present the good news of Jesus for living our daily lives and as a way to escape eternal torment. Jesus accepted the penalty to die so that we might have life and have it more abundantly because He loves us.

Some people pray to God for financial blessings and wait for Him to bless them. But when they receive their blessings, they become so high and mighty with a little money under their booth strap. Some are impossible to communicate with because they feel that they have arrived. Perhaps God has to bless them in measurement at His set time to keep them from destroying themselves.

There was a young man, a newborn Christian, and God blessed him with a new vehicle. This young man mishandled his blessing. He stopped attending church for a length of time. He chose his vehicle over serving the Lord. He drove around flaunting his vehicle instead of driving his new car to church to learn more about how-to walk-in victory and continue to receive God's blessings. He chose to be cold instead of hot. God said, "I rather you are hot or cold but not lukewarm." Cold people accept Christ and choose to follow their own path after receiving salvation. Hot people accept Christ and choose to be on fire for the Lord and follow the path of Jesus. Lukewarm people accept Christ and choose to follow Christ when it is convenient. They are Godly one minute and worldly the next minute.

Does it make sense that you are rewarded for obedience and chastening for disobedience? Absolutely, for instance, in the natural, you asked your daughter to cook a meal and your son to mow the lawn. The daughter cooks a delicious meal, and the son decides to hang out with his friends. The parents reward their daughter, and the son is grounded for his noncompliance. The supernatural has the same similarity. One person accepts the Lord and strives to follow God's plans and direction. The other person accepts the Lord and decides to follow his or her own plans and direction. We must choose either/or because you cannot love both simultaneously. You must make a choice to love God and hate the enemy. It is just that simple.

Some people receive a healing from God, and they are not appreciative enough to thank Him for their healing. They continue in their sin. When a Christian continues in sin, it shows a misunderstanding of God's grace and mercy in their lives and subjects them to chastening. When an unrighteous continues in sin until death, the Bible says, they will not inherit the kingdom of God.

Jesus healed a man and told the man he was healed to go and sin no more. He is saying the same thing today. The amazing dimension of this story, Jesus did nothing to bring glory to Himself. In all things, He glorified the Father. There are countless people who help others and steer away from trying to get adoration for what they have done. We should always "pay it forward" by giving back to someone else without looking for a return.

Some people question why God has not given them certain blessings that they have petitioned for over an extended period of time. It is not that God refuses to bless them, but when He gives us blessings, He moves in His timing. Ten years seems like an exceptionally long time in humans' timeline. I know because I worked an extra ten years beyond my desired plan at the sewing factory. However, ten years can be just one day in God's eyes. Previously, in this chapter, I said that God is not bound by time. When He gives us blessings, He wants us to make effective use of our blessings by sharing them with the less fortunate, as well as furthering the kingdom of God.

God said He has a plan for our lives. So, when He blesses us in our planned season, we must be wise in our choices. Carelessness could have a similar result as the young man who did not know how to cultivate his blessing. Sometimes, we get caught up in this worldly cycle, where materialistic things become more important than the things of God. You might say: "well, I know I can manage any blessings that God gives me; I am a seasoned believer in God's Word." Well, seasoned believer, have you ever missed the mark with a particular blessing God has given you? Did you fail to cultivate the blessing? Did you mismanage your gift? If we are truly honest, we all can attest to making errors in our lives related to what God has given to us and commanded of us.

Many times, we have preferred to follow our own desires. This is where grace and repentance abound. Some people assume that it is meaningless to repent because grace covers it all. When breaking the word *assume* down into three syllables and changing the first three words of assume to *fool* instead of using the actual word, which is a slang curse word. The word can be translated as a fool. Therefore, the devil makes a "Fool-U-Me" when we assume anything. The enemy often uses his assumed device to manipulate God's people.

Again, we are not perfect; we are going to make errors on this journey as Christians as we wait for Jesus to return. This is while repentance and grace are necessary because they assist you in making a change of any actions that are not like God. Having a change of mind and heart will cause you to turn away from the wrong and embrace the right way of life.

It would be wise to let our sins go before us and not trail behind us into heaven because every human will be accountable for the things they have done on the earth. If it goes before us, we have asked God to forgive us. If they trailed behind us, then there was no repentance. This is why it is so important to repent.

God has reserved special blessings for those who appreciate their blessings, are willing to share with others and live according to God's righteousness. There are numerous people walking by faith that their blessing season is in progress, but patience is the key. God has a set time for everything, and He is always right on time. He has given us His Word to live by and to have some sense of knowledge of the future, but He has never given us the discernment to fully understand what He does. Some things are a mystery. If we are as knowledgeable as God and can perform just as perfectly as God, then we would be God. We know this is impossible because we did not create ourselves. The most important thing we can do is accept His son, be happy, and do the best that we can while we are still alive on earth. We must remember when our burdens get too heavy, He will carry us in His loving arms over to the other side. We have to depend on Him for our very next breath, so we must express our dependency by waiting patiently for Him to deliver us from any test or trial we might endure. He will come at His set time, and it will be right on time!

I have to briefly mention the pandemic. We realized, especially between 2020 -2021, that this dreadful virus certainly brought much confusion, pain, death, and inflation. One lesson we all can benefit from this is a better understanding of what it means to wait upon the Lord. Our lives were put on hold, and trusting in the Lord was our only option. He was in control then, and He will continue to be in control because He is the only wise and sufficient God.

CHAPTER TWO
Born A Sinner

As human beings, we all have different opinions of the Bible and our own perceptions of what makes a person a sinner. A selected number of people believe that violation of any of the Ten Commandments makes an individual a sinner. It is impossible for mere humans not to commit sin. According to the Word of God, we all have sinned in this world.

A baby born into this world is a sinner by nature. It makes no difference if the baby was born by an unwed mother or any other sin. No matter how humans enter into this world, once born, we are sinners. We all became sinners because Adam and Eve disobeyed God's Commandments. If you do not believe in God, Jesus Christ, or the Holy Spirit, there is no way you can receive this message because you probably believe that you are self-made or some other life form. Those who do believe in God, Jesus Christ, and the Holy Spirit can agree that Adam and Eve are the reason everyone is identified as a sinner when they are born into this world.

Certain people believe that anyone who has done something wrong according to moral law makes them a sinner. This only indicates that you sinned, which we are all capable of doing. No matter how considerate we are or how generous we are in giving, we all entered into the world as sinners.

Countless people believe that if you commit adultery or fornication, you are a sinner. But this is not exactly true for those who have accepted Christ as Lord and Savior. Believers of Christ just sinned and need to repent, which is godly sorrow. They must ask Christ to forgive them of their sins and be determined not to commit that act of sin again. The different between Christians and non-Christians is that once a person accepts Jesus Christ as their personal Savior, they are no longer a sinner. This does not mean that they do not sin. Let me attempt to explain: believers have an advocate, 'Jesus,' to speak on their behalf when they sin. He makes a request to the Father to forgive them. Sinners do not have an advocate, but we all have an adversary, 'Satan,' that endeavors to destroy us daily.

Some people say that they speak directly to God. This is impossible because they cannot bypass His son. God said no man can come to Him unless they come by way of His son. This is why the older generation says that such prayers did not go any further than the ceiling. However, do not misread this because God can bless whomever and whenever He pleases.

There is good news for sinners; they do not have to remain sinners for the rest of their lives just because they were born sinners. It is safe to say it can be a temporary condition because there is an escape, and that escape is coming into the knowledge of salvation which I will explain in deeper depth later in this chapter.

The reason everyone sins, Christians and non-Christians, is because the adversary is constantly influencing us to do evil deeds. It is fundamental that parents teach their children at an early age how to tell the truth. After a child has been taught to tell the truth, he or she has a choice to admit the truth or continue to tell a lie. That is why it is so important to train a child in the admiration of the Lord to instill in them godly principles.

I was watching a cartoon movie on television with my threeyear-old God-sent granddaughter. The father sneaked into the kitchen and ate a piece of cake. The mother asked the father, "did you eat the cake?" He said, "no." Then, the mother sneaked into the kitchen and ate a cookie. The father asked the mother, "did you eat the cookie?" She said, "no." The small child sneaked into the kitchen and ate a bowl of ice cream. The mother asked the small child, "did you eat the ice cream?" the child said, "no." They all lied, and my three-year-old God-sent granddaughter, Maleyn, jumped up and down on the couch, saying, "no! no! no!" She was shouting "no" alone with the dishonest cartoon characters. I must ask you, was this cartoon teaching this child how to lie, or was this cartoon teaching a three-year-old that people lie? To be honest, the flesh indulges in the pleasure of wrongdoing, even in a small child, because sin is the groundwork for being disobedient to God's way of living. The majority of the time, society teaches us moral ethics in this world, which assist us in making good decisions - but not godly decisions.

God, in His divine wisdom, empowers us to live in this world using our common senses to know right from wrong. Godly wisdom assists us daily as well in making sound judgments in practical matters. His divine wisdom also aids us in academic learning to help us to understand the world in which we live.

When we live a life of sin, the enemy will use us as bait to perform evil attacks to destroy other human beings. It is imperative that non-believers make the most important decision of their lives to change their lifestyle from a sinner to a believer because humans' fight is not against any physical enemy. It is against demonic strategy and demonic power where the enemy twists the Word of God and seeks to control unsaved people. Unsaved people do not have the power as born-again believers who have the Holy Ghost abiding within them.

However, these demonic powers will use their influence to weaken Christians' faith and cause the Christians to indulge in sinful behaviors. That is why Christians must always have the Word of God ready to fight the enemy constantly.

An unsaved person can reverse the attack of demonic powers against them by reconciling their lives back to God through His son, Jesus Christ. Reconciliation gives access to the power of God to rebuke these evil spirits when they endeavor to attack. However, make no mistake about it: we are saved by grace, and we are not going to be perfect; however, we must strive to live according to God's Word.

On another note, my deceased auntie often said, "We are supposed to cry when a child is born into the world and laugh when someone dies." But we do the opposite because when a child comes into the world, we are happy, and we are laughing from ear to ear. But when a loved one dies, we are crying and grieving over them constantly. The reason she said this is because when a child is born, he or she has entered into a sinful world. When we die in the Lord, we are departing from a sinful world.

God's Word tells us that Paradise is for the regenerate man and Hades for the unregenerate man. God is so divine that He gives us free will to choose. We can follow our own path or the path of Jesus. God wants us to come to Him because we love Him without being forced to love Him. There are people in this world today who cannot commit to following Jesus. They do not want to give up their lifestyle. Once you give your life to Christ, the old man must die, and you become a new creature.

Myth: *Once you accept Jesus as your personal savior, an individual is placed under the radar, and anything you do that is ungodly, you are no longer saved.* This is truly a myth because once you are a true believer you cannot reverse your salvation except for one reason, and I will discuss that reason later in this chapter.

Jesus said, "I am married to the backslider." Backslider indicates that you have fallen away and have converted to pre-conversion habits. Falling back into a sinful lifestyle means that you have completely turned away from God to pursue your own desires. Even though you have chosen the ways of sinners, He is saying there is no room for a divorce. However, there will be consequences for your actions. This is why the Bible states, "many are weak and sick.' God is not in the business of giving us a gift and taking it back like humans do. If you are reluctant to respond the way someone wants you to, you can easily be kicked to the curb. However, Christians must remember that we are covered by grace, unearned and undeserved, and this is a gift from the almighty God.

My beloved late Bishop Ritchie often said, "this really takes people time to grasp because it sounds like a free ticket to sin." This is not a free ticket to sin; this is a bride who has lost the Christian's way and needs to return to the groom to gain back his or her rightful fellowship with the Lord because they have backslidden by entertaining the enemies' devices.

What if a bride does not return to the groom and dies in his or her sin? If a backslider does not repent and dies, it is God's decision on their final resting place. Humans are not the judge or the jury of people's resting place. I once heard a person say, "my son was a backslider, and he did not make it back in, and he is gone to hell." Everyone has his or her own opinion or the way they perceive what the Word of God said about a situation like this. My opinion again, God has the last word on a person's eternal resting place, not humans.

However, I implore you to have a change of heart this day. If you are not saved or a backslider, do not walk away from God and lose your rightful place in the Lord because the Bible definitely says you will be judged by God accordingly. Believers who recognize that Jesus is their anchor live a better life. That is why it is important for believers to keep their eyes on Jesus and not on people.

Some people may think they have arrived, but we are all just *a drop in the bucket*. A drop in the bucket is just a small amount when standing next to the one who died for our sins. Do not jump off the ship if things do not go your way; stand firm on God's Word. I am making a request to all backsliders: return home and stay faithful to God so that you can receive what is rightfully yours. To the unsaved, I entreat you to receive the gift of salvation today, so your name is written in the Book of Life.

The key to your final designation is that you have truly accepted Jesus into your heart with true repentance. There are only two witnesses: Jesus and you. Jesus took our sins upon Himself and paid for them in full, and when we believe that He died for the ungodly, it gives Him permission to rule over us through His Word. We are forever His.

Now let us discuss the unpardonable sin; God said, "I forgive you of every sin that you committed except blasphemy." The only reason you can lose your salvation is blasphemy against the Holy Spirit. People will be forgiven for every sin, but blasphemy against the Holy Spirit will not be forgiven. The Bible said, "if you speak against the Holy Spirit in this age and the age to come, it is an unforgivable sin." Please remember, being a sinner is reversable, and speaking in vain against God's son is reversable. But let us not forget that speaking against the Holy Spirit is non-reversable.

As a believer, we want to give tribute to the one who created us, saved us, gifted us, and lives in us. He deserves our crowns by striving to live a holy life. This is the confession to obtain our heavenly home with God and accept Christ as our Lord and Savior. The things that must transpire are *BELIEVE, MOUTH,* and *HEART.* Believe God's Word that Jesus is Lord, open your mouth and confess you are a sinner in need of His forgiveness, and accept Him into your heart to indicate acceptance of God's forgiveness. Then allow His Word to cleanse your heart, and from that day forward, acknowledge Him in everything.

Take everything the master has prepared for you, a well-made weapon of the best material -His Word - and put it to use so you will be able to stand tall in this cruel world.

CHAPTER THREE
God Orchestrate Lives

Life consists of giving something back to the world through selfexpression and changing our attitude when we are presented with a situation or circumstance that we cannot change. This is where we, as human beings, have to respond to the creator, God. God has a purpose in creating us. We are not born knowing our purpose. This is why we must ask God what our purpose is in this world.

We need to take a thorough look at our lives and begin to recognize our negative behaviors and habits. For instance, we have negative habits that we refuse to let go of because if we let go of them, it will make us feel vulnerable. We keep walls up to defend ourselves to prevent being hurt by others.

Publishing this book is huge for me because the enemy spoke more than he has ever spoken in months. Some of the things the enemy said, "Who is going to read this book? There are known qualified people who are authors, but you are a nobody. I know you are not going to put that in this book?" I had to take authority over the deceptive spirit by shutting down every negative thought that was presented. It is a requirement as believers to protect our peace and joy.

God has purposes for all of His children, and He vows to fulfill those purposes. He needs willing vessels to step out of their comfort zone and let Him navigate them through it.

Returning to college in my sixties to get a Bachelor of Science degree in sociology and authoring this book was definitely out of my comfort zone. Some of the things that kept me motivated while I was freewriting were family and friends who inquired about the progress of the book. The Sunday sermons at Giving God the Praise

Ministries by our pastor, Terrance Watkins, kept me motivated as well.

However, there are quite a few things in this world that will take you out of your comfort zone. But you have to let the Lord steer you through them. Without Him, it is impossible to complete any assignments within your own strength.

Some individuals might say there is a colossal of people who are not saved and have accomplished many things in this world. They are billionaires and millionaires who have reputable lifestyles and great success. However, if Jesus does not order their steps in building their houses, then the houses were built in vain. Believers have to depend on Jesus to meet their every needs, not money. Do not misunderstand what I am implying because money is a requirement in this world. It is the love of money wherein sin flourishes. We must let God orchestrate His purpose in our lives because He has a unique, tailor-made plan for it. The work God has for believers might begin behind the scenes; however, God will reveal His purpose in His precise time.

We must act on God's plan because God cannot be hindered. He is directing our lives to an ultimate end, and His favor is one of the greatest blessings a believer can have. He is sovereignly able to orchestrate the events of our lives eternally. Our faith is to trust Him and be committed to His tailored-made plan that He has assigned.

To follow His plan is similar to when you put an address into your navigation system. If you make a premature turn, the voice connected to the speaker from the navigation system will say, "You have left the plan." I implore you do not leave the plan of God. If this should happen, make a U-turn and get back on course. Let Him continue to take you safely to the destination that He has chosen for you. To have successful results, we should embrace His purpose and let Him direct our paths. The only thing God is asking a believer is to have faith in Him.

Some people hesitate to surrender to Jesus because it will alter their lifestyles, and that is scary to them. I understand that changes are scary, but refusing to change a depraved lifestyle is scarier. You must open your mouth and tell the Lord that you are willing to stop following your own desires and embrace His purpose. Remember, whatever you are endeavoring to accomplish, it is a failure if Christ is not orchestrating it.

We have to deny ourselves and follow Jesus because living a life cut off from Christ is very exhausting. Attempting to act okay when you are not okay is frustrating. There are so many people who are running here and there without meaningful purpose on the earth.

Many avoid their purpose because they are afraid of the unknown. You have to trust God in the process by allowing Him to orchestrate your life. Some people limit themselves in what they can accomplish because their faith is deactivated, and their feelings are activated. It should be the reverse. Our faith should be activated and our feelings deactivated. Feelings have a way of revealing unhealthy choices, and feelings can also cause you to temporarily escape the purpose that God has ordained for you before the beginning of time. God is in control, and His purpose will not fail.

There are some people who believe that denial of their feelings helps them remain in control; however, their feelings will eventually control them. This is why so many children and young people are committing suicide. They are trying to handle things themselves. We all need direction and guidance to reach our potential goals in life. It is so vital that adults reach out to these children and young adults. We must have listening ears to hear what they are sharing from their perspective. Then -in turn, we must share the gospel with them because the gospel is spreading the good news, which is never hurtful news. As adults, we should always motivate and promote the Lord in our lives, not recognition of self.

There are many people who seek recognition for themselves by hiding behind the Bible to manipulate others. The only place Christ sought recognition or approval was from His Father. When a person seeks recognition for himself or herself, they are choosing to let gossip shine rather than the gospel shine.

Self-seekers want all the recognition from people. I am not trying to belittle anyone. I am endeavoring to explain the difference between gospel and gossip so you can be aware of an individual attempting to shower you with gossip of others instead of the gospel of Jesus Christ. It is very important to read God's Word for yourself.

Furthermore, do not be drawn into or deceived when the gossip is hidden with a prayer request such as "We need to pray for Humpty because Dumpty took his wife?" I used these names to avoid identifying individuals.

Unquestionably, this person just called to spread some hot mess. The bottom line is that the individual was not endeavoring to support the person but to expose them. The prayer was never included in the conversation, which was supposed to have been the reason for the call in the beginning.

The Word of God has taught me how to stop an individual from presenting gossip because I realize I am a partaker of the foolishness by listening to it. I am accountable for my actions, even if I did not comment on this uncomfortable conversation. I allowed the person to pour unpleasant oil into my spiritual cup.

Sometimes, we just refuse to submit to the plan that God has orchestrated for our lives. My birth father died when I was a teenager. My mother died when I was one year old. I was reminiscing about both of them, but particularly about my father. He would share God's Word with his children when we were very small kids. He said, "The Lord called me to the ministry to preach, but I refused." He ran from ministry because he did not want to give up his lifestyle of drinking alcohol and having intimate relationships with women. When he became intoxicated, he would summon us together to sit down and hear him preach the Word of God. In other words, he could not escape God's calling because God instilled a deep desire in his spirit to share His Word.

I heard a spiritual person once say, "Do not do as I do, but do as I say." I realized after God saved me that it is the deliverers' and the receivers' responsibility to live according to God's Word. The Word of God tells us to do more than just speak the Word. We must also be hearers of the Word. For that reason, the deliverer must abide by the Word of God that he or she speaks, and the receiver must abide by the Word of God that he or she hears.

We thought our father was just entertaining us and did not believe what he was preaching. We were secretly making fun of him because he was intoxicated. He continued to preach intoxicated until he passed away.

My siblings and I did not accept Jesus during that era. Many of my siblings are deceased, but those who are alive today are saved and sharing the Word of God.

When God puts purpose in you, it is not just for you but for your children and your children's children. After my children were married and had their own families, I became a foster parent for a number of years to give love and provide for those who needed a caring environment. They are now adults and have their own families. We are in touch with a few of our foster children. My husband and I still encourage them in life challenges.

When God puts purpose in you, it is time to get out of the shadow of water and follow the leading of the Spirit of God. When Jesus told the fishermen to throw their nets out into the deep, they followed His instructions. Suppose those fishermen had stood on the fact that they had thrown their nets out there and were not going to throw them again because they had not caught anything. They would have missed a bounteous catch of fish by being disobedient.

Remember this: being obedient is necessary to receive godly blessings.

When I retired, the enemy tried to put fear in me by injecting negative beliefs into my thoughts. During the enemy's maneuvering on the earth, he used trickery and deceptive devices. He said, "If you transition to retirement, your life is going to go down the drain. You better keep your work status; do not let anybody fool you; you are going to have a rough time." He was attempting to keep me bound and fearful. The enemy was attempting to stop me from the confirmation of peace that I received from the Lord to retire. It was God's set time for me to launch out into the deep, and it was right on time. My husband, Harold, and I have been blessed abundantly since we retired.

The devil was attempting to impart counterfeit counseling, which is a false comfort. Counterfeit means an imposter, in other words, just a phony spirit. The opposite of the counterfeit is the true comforter, the Holy Spirit that will guide you into all truth.

I believe it would be more favorable to walk in the likeness of Christ instead of receiving a temporary counterfeit comfort. When we choose counterfeit comforts, we are deceived because we think that we are getting something real, and that will bring true satisfaction. However, the fulfillment always comes up short. For instance, you find a man to marry you because you are in desperate need of a spouse. God's Word says, "When a man finds a wife, he has found a treasure." It does not tell women to go and search for a husband and often get a counterfeit. Do not misinterpret this because God can speak to the woman and inform her that a particular man is to be her husband. Then, she must put herself in his way to find a good thing.

I told my husband that when he found me, he found a good thing and that I was a gift from God to bring him love and joy with pleasure. I did not want a counterfeit man, and I am sure he did not want a counterfeit woman. Counterfeit people lure others in by hanging bait. This is much like a fish seeking food. Once the person is hooked, the illusion becomes clear, and now the person is hanging on that hook, thirsty for love and waiting for the pretender to take them off the hook, which is probably not going to happen.

In the spirit realm, God gives us a choice to choose the counterfeit comfort or receive the Holy Spirit. The counterfeit comfort takes the edge off your problems temporarily, but the Holy Spirit can deliver you forever. Only Jesus can touch that place in us and leave us with something that is everlasting. Our emotional holes cannot be filled with anything else, but God. God is offering us a better way by accepting His son. You must let God send you a husband without going through the counterfeit search.

Although God gives us free will to follow our own path, I urge you to make sure to use that free will pass wisely. There is nothing or nobody who can fill the thirst that you are craving. Only the Son of God can fill that emptiness that you are feeling. However, when we are empty and starving for love or just to have someone to say they love us, it makes us feel wanted. This is how people settle for that temporary counterfeit comfort because they want to feel loved. Have you ever heard people say I know it is wrong, but I just got to have it?

I was married to my children's father; we were having some major problems. I was a sinner who needed a Savior. After being married for a few years, I accepted Jesus Christ. But my husband refused to walk that path. We were going through financial problems and issues with infidelity. A godly mentor advised me that I needed to pray the fervent prayer that God would draw him to His son so that he would give his life to Christ. I had to pray what I call the S and S prayer, which was God giving me the grace to *stay* or the *strength* to leave. There was one person who gave me some crazy advice: a piece of man was better than having no man. I realize that a piece of a man is a man who shirks his responsibility as a husband and a father.

There were issues beyond my ability to make it right; only God has the power to resolve them. We have to realize that we cannot change another human being. No amount of investment can change a person who avoids godly counsel. You have to ask God to help you change your shortcomings and pray that your spouse seeks the Lord for his or her own inadequacies. Especially if an unsaved spouse wishes to dwell with his or her saved spouse, we all have areas in a relationship that we must personally work toward correcting. However, if that unsaved spouse wishes not to stay with their saved spouse, you must let them depart. This is exactly what happened in my relationship. After many years of being single, I married a God-fearing man, and he loves me regardless of my flaws. I am a God-fearing woman, and I love my husband regardless of his flaws as well.

However, when a soul is hungry, it will look to anything to take the edge off and fill that void. I say to you this day that only Jesus can fill that void, whether you are married or single. No other human being or thing can do it. One can receive a mate, and this mate can enhance your life, but only Jesus can give you the fulfillment that will last forever. Allow Jesus to fill that void because we are living in times of uncertainty.

Trust God to give you a husband or wife, and do not worry about the clock ticking. I trusted the Lord to give me a husband, and after many years of being single, He blessed me with the man of my dreams. God paired me with a man who reveres Him and loves me. God can be humorous! My prayer to God was to send me Mr. Right, and his last name is Wright. I knew my husband, Harold, was directly from God. We have a wonderful relationship. Do we have misunderstandings off and on? Of course, we do. I remember we were returning from a road trip, and we were talking in a loud and aggressive voice to each other about the direction. My brother Michael and his daughter were in the backseat. She turned to her father and said, "Daddy, they are fussing." My husband and I turned and looked at our backseat passengers and said, " We do not fuss; we discuss." The vehicle was filled with an outburst of laughter.

I implore you to wait on the Lord, no matter how long it takes. God will always be there to shower down His marriage blessings on you, and it will be right on time!

There are some women and men who do not desire to be married. Some people prefer to live alone, and some prefer to be roomies.
Remember what I said: use your free pass wisely because God's Word is His approval.

We do not want to be like Esau. If we settle for temporary counterfeit blessings from the evil one, our dreams will be stolen, and our lives will be encamped in a cycle that enslaves us. We do not want to alter our future by selling our peace for a temporary relief of a counterfeit, false comfort. Ponder this, we have much more than Esau. We have the Holy Spirit. If you do not have it, it is a free gift from God. Just ask Him for your free gift as a child of God.

Some people say that they have the Holy Spirit, but they have not accepted Christ as their personal Savior. The Holy Spirit does not reside in a person who has not accepted Christ. When you accept Jesus as your personal Savior, you receive God's Spirit. However, to receive the Fire Baptism of the Holy Spirit is a gift from God where His power is an overcomer. Let us also clear up some misunderstandings about speaking in tongues. Speaking in tongues is evidence that you have the Holy Spirit. For instance, two people are sitting side by side, and they do not know if the person sitting next to them has the gift of the Holy Spirit until they speak in tongues. The Holy Spirit is speaking in a cloven tongue, which is a gift that is given to a person directly from God. It is the purification that does the cleansing work in us. Through this power, we are able to break the bondages of evil forces that attempt to destroy us.

When I received the gift of the Holy Spirit, my life changed drastically. I received power over things that I could not control beforehand. I learned to lean on the Holy Spirit to guide me by stepping aside, standing back, taking my hands off of my life, and letting the Spirit of Truth do the work through me. He will meet our needs and fill our emptiness. Whatever our emptiness is, the cycle will break, and we will be able to live with the freedom we have always hoped to be possible.

In Christ, we can avoid trying to deal with our problems. We must step back and let Him guide us into victory because we have complete freedom in Him. We are more than conquerors in Christ.

We must be willing to let God orchestrate our lives. We are at a turning point in our lives because everything has come upon the earth. God has put purpose in us from the beginning of time. We must be willing to follow His plan all the way to the finish line.

CHAPTER FOUR
P.O.T. Experiences

There are different types of pots, for instance, a crock pot in which we can slow cook different types of delicious meals such as beef stew, ham hocks and collard greens, black eye peas, and so on. Some people used urine pots. Then there are pot pies full of delicious vegetables, beef, turkey, or chicken with a crust. Also, some people use a crackpot to consume illegal drugs into their bodies.

P.O.T. is the acronym for Passing Our Test. This is the P.O.T. I would like to share this with you because as we go through this journey of life, we will definitely have some chaos, issues, problems, challenges, tests and trials until Jesus' return. Hopefully, after reading this chapter, it will help us to pass our tests more gracefully. Some people go through the same tests and trials over and over again until they actually pass their spiritual tests. It is similar to our familiar academic tests. If we fail a test in class, in most cases, we are given the opportunity to take it again.

Moving forward, when we encounter challenges and issues in our lives, our full trust has to be centered in the Lord. We cannot lean on our own understanding in the matter; we must reference Christ to direct our path especially if we are grace babies. Grace babies are saved through faith. Grace is not of us, but it is the gift of God. We cannot boast about it because we did not take any part in it; it is God's grace.

We must remember that we are more spiritual beings than natural beings. God designed the body to house our spirit and soul. The flesh strives to be in control because the enemy converses with our soul to get it to agree with the body to fulfill the desires of the flesh. However, the Spirit of God will always guide us in the right direction. Consequently, in all honesty, occasionally, I have missed the Holy Spirit in doing the honorable thing. I have listened to my own voice and suggested to my own soul that it was God speaking to me because I was enticed by something that I wanted. I tried to convince myself that it was alright. But God was nowhere in that mess. This is why I am so thankful to God for repentance grace which gives me the opportunity to reclaim my rightful place in Him.

Permit me to insert this in reference to voices. There are different types of voices there is God's voice, Satanic voice, and our voice. Satan comes as an angel of light to deceive us, and if we are not careful, we might believe that it is God speaking. Every spirit that you hear speaking to you is not God's voice. To distinguish God's voice from Satan's, we must be able to discern the diverse voices. God speaks through His written word, "logos" wherein His promises abide in His grace and mercy. Also, His "rhema" word is a spoken Word of God that is personally applied to a person's life. He also speaks through visions, dreams, and prophecies. Prophecies must line up with the Word of God. If you receive anything contrary to His Holy Word, then it is more likely demonic voices that sound like Jesus or a spiritual leader because these are voices that we trust.

Satan has his limitations, but the almighty creator, God, is unlimited. If you have received the Holy Spirit, He will speak to you and bring God's Word back to your remembrance and guide you in all things. I urge you to receive your gift from God because the deceiving spirits are always in action from the devil and demons.

The enemy's occupation is to deceive God's people. When you stay in tune with the Holy Spirit, He will alert your spirit of the enemy's deceptive attacks. I am warning you: do not listen to every voice that speaks to you. Do not trust that it is God speaking. When God speaks to us, it will be substantiated in His set time, but do not twiddle your thumbs impatiently while waiting for an answer. It takes patience when we are waiting for the Lord to answer prayers.

A person has the choice to live virtuously through the Word of God. That person must determine whether he or she is willing to conform to the Word of God. Christians are called to a life of obedience by hearing the Word of God and acting on it. There are persuasive dark spirits that tempt people to not walk according to God's Word. Some people let a lot of things cloud their minds and play on their emotions. These types of influential spirits will cause people not to pass their test.

In the Bible, God instructed Abram to get away from where he lived and his kindred. Abram certainly passed one part of the test by moving away, but he failed the other part because he took one of his relatives- his nephew-Lot. He also took his wife Sarai, which was expected because when a couple is married, they are one. If we really want the full result of God's blessings, we must follow the entire instruction and not alter it. For instance, my friend asked me to go with her to select and purchase a vehicle. We did not find a vehicle. A month later, my friend's spouse accompanied her to buy a vehicle, and they bought a brand-new vehicle. She stopped by my home to show her blessing. She informed me that she had been disobedient to God because He told her to take her spouse. I replied, "You should have said that in the beginning. I would have never attended a vehicle search with you." I was distraught because I felt that I was a distraction. We must be real with ourselves and others because honesty is another key to your blessings. Her blessing was delayed because she did not follow God's instructions. I was agitated because I felt responsible. However, most importantly, she received her vehicle blessing, and I got over my flustered feelings.

At some point and time, we all have altered the plan that God designed for us. We have left the plan by mistake and sometimes deliberately. But God, in His goodness and mercy, gives us the opportunity to recalibrate. Sometimes, we reach a point in life where we gradually drift off course from the plan that God has designed for us, and this causes us to fail our test. Periodically, we need a fresh jumpstart to get back on track. We must make a U-turn immediately when we realize our own plans attempt to overthrow God's plan for our lives. Leaving the plan of God can cause many tests and trials in our lives that drain us naturally and spiritually. Tests and trials teach us that we definitely need a Savior to maneuver through life because, without a savior, we are fair game for the devil's devices. We are easy targets for the enemy to destroy us. Make no mistakes about it; the enemy knows the real believers from the imposters. It is vital that we are in covenant with the Lord until Jesus returns.

We have to face pots one step at a time. As we go through these tests, we cannot ride the roller coaster with our hands up in the air, screaming as we go up and down and all around when we are experiencing pots.

These tests move so fast-one after another that sometimes it feels like we are on a rolling coaster with fire blazing from it. My philosophy is when an individual has been set on fire by the devil, you must use the three second rule, which is stop, drop, and roll. *Stop* represents God; let the enemy know who you serve and what your status is, which is a child of the most high God. You are a chosen vessel of God, you belong to God, you have a right to the throne of God, and His Word is the blueprint that you live by. *Drop* represents Jesus. He died for your sins, and He is your Lord and Savior. You must give thanks to Him, rejoice in Him, and abide in Him, and He will give you the victory, not once but every time. *Roll* represents the Holy Spirit that guides you through every test and trial that you encounter. He teaches you how to overcome your tests and trials. He will instruct you on a daily basis.

One of the ministers at our church related that we are under attack and that we have a target on our backs. I strongly urge you to remember the three second rule when you have a target on your back.

During your pot, there may be days when you have a pity- party, but do not stay down, retreat, and move forward. I have learned that the way I respond to the pot can have a significant effect on whether it becomes a roadblock in my life or a highway to maximize my speed. Whichever one forges, I will continue to persevere toward joy and happiness.

According to "**compassioninternational.com**," joy is an inner feeling, and happiness is an outward expression. Joy endures hardship and trials and connects with meaning and purpose. A person can pursue happiness but always choose joy. So, remember to pursue happiness, but when it is all said and done, choose joy. Do not give your own power to the enemy because he will take full advantage of it and use it against you in whatever you are attempting to achieve in life.

It is important to ask this question when you are going through pot: "Is this a test from God or an attack from Satan?" Satan's results lead to pain and death. Remember, whenever or whatever test you go through, God is aware of it. Whenever you are going through pots, God wants you to call on His son, Jesus, because He is the only one who can deliver you.

God allows sin, but He is not the author of sin. He gives His permission for anything to occur in life. Remember the story of Job in the Bible. Satan had to ask God for permission to touch Job's life and Job's belongings. Do not get it twisted; the devil is not in control. The controllability that Satan has over God's people is the capacity that God allows him to undertake.

The Devil is a created being by God, and God allowed Satan some control over the earth's atmosphere. This is why he is the prince of the power of the air. God is eternal, and He controls the entire universe and everything in it. He will use a trial from the enemy to test your faith and bring about spiritual growth in your life. If Satan bombards you with enough trials, you will seek the Lord. I can say that is a true factor because I did. I accepted Jesus as my Lord and savior when I realized nobody or nothing else could take away the pain that I was experiencing. Had I refused to accept Jesus as my personal Savior, then Satan's attempt to direct my path would have been a successful mission in my life.

Remember this when we are going through our pots: we must determine if we are being tested by God or attacked by enemy.

CHAPTER FIVE
Neck-Turning Blessings

There is no doubt that God has the power and authority to bless His people. He grants approval and permission for a person to be blessed by others as well. God enhances their walk with Him and elevates them to a position to receive a neck-turning blessing.

My definition of a neck-turning blessing is when God shows an individual extraordinary favoritism, and he or she has no doubt that it came directly from God. When this person walks or drives past another person, it will prompt the other person's neck to turn immediately in the direction of the extraordinarily favored person. They acknowledge the blessings of the Lord in that person's life.

Blessings from God are a joyful state for those who find their purpose and fulfillment in Him. To be blessed by God is the best life obtainable for those who love, revere, and order their lives according to God's Word. The reason some people might not receive God's blessings as He has designed is because they are speaking negatively about themselves and their families. God spoke life into existence, and we can speak life into our own situations and not death.

It is very important that we realize we give life to what we say, good or bad. For instance, when we are saying things contrary to God's Word, such as, " I do not think my husband is going to make it through this surgery, or I am going to get kicked out of my home soon." We are setting ourselves up for a huge fall. We cannot talk about defeat and expect victory. Nor can we talk lack and expect abundance. When we are constantly talking negatively, we are prophesying our future.

If we want to be the recipient of a neck-turning blessing, then we cannot speak or think negative thoughts continuously. Notice, I said *continuously* because we are going to make slip-ups here and there because we have not received our glorified body. We have not reached perfection, and we must continue to strive for excellence until the bridegroom returns.

The Word of God says, "There are life and death in the power of the tongue." I urge you to remember God's Word when you get ready to speak something contrary to righteousness. As my cousin, Shugg, who is no longer with us on earth, would say, "Zip it." Do not speak it, and if the negative thought comes to your mind, dismiss it right away. Think of something good, something lovely, and something that has worth.

When we are struggling with insecure feelings, brokenness, loneliness, rejection, and feeling left behind, these feelings are not from God. They are from the liar and the father of lies, the devil. The Word of God plainly shows us how to be free from these kinds of chains by identifying who we are in Christ Jesus. When the enemy tries to label you with ungodly things, you must renew your mind with whom God says you are.

You are in His beloved Son and remember to always identify yourself with the Son of God. When the enemy comes with a false identity, let your faith kick in and put the enemy on the run by giving him the true identity of who you are. Speak from your gut and believe it in your heart: "I am a new creation, I am loved, I am justified, I am completely forgiven, I am a temple in which God dwells, and I am God's favorite." That is how neck-turning blessings work because you know who you are in Christ Jesus.

I went to renew my car tag years ago and I asked for a personalized tag engraved, *'Highly Favored.'* The clerk informed me that someone had already purchased that name. I told the clerk I was going to step out of line and think of another name. As I was about to step out of line, my spirit bore witness to the Holy Spirit that immediately said, "You are at the top of the line as one of God's favorites." I told the clerk that I had changed my mind about stepping out of line and that I had the exact name that I wanted to be engraved on my tag, *Topfavor,* because I have preferential favor from God.

My sister Margaret's quote is, "I know what time it is." When you know what time it is in God, then you can walk in His favor. We have to take it up a notch: the enemy is destroying God's people. Most of the time, because they are feeling unworthy, and the reason they are feeling unworthy is due to the occasional sin that the devil constantly brings to the minds of Christians. However, Christians must remember that they do not have their glorified bodies; therefore, they will sometimes fall short of God's requirements.

We must know who we are in Christ and be aware of the devil's devices. Some people have a lack of knowledge of who they are because they have not paired natural knowledge with supernatural knowledge. We must upload God's Word into our soul and meditate on it day and night to release supernatural knowledge in order to gain access to God's faith and wisdom.

Believers must seek the Master's heart and stay focused and connected to the problem solver. Make sure we do not get caught up in this worldly system. Above all, we must have faith in God and trust the process. God's Word tells us He will never leave us nor forsake us. We must be all-in because a whole-hearted Savior is not interested in half- hearted followers.

When it comes to our walk with the Lord, repentance allows us to refine, which means to improve our walk. This will re-define us and create opportunities for building a stronger relationship with God and His people. We must repent when we err because repentance is not for God; repentance is for us. If you are not saved by grace, you have the opportunity to become a grace baby. Review Chapter Two, *Born a Sinner,* and follow God's instruction to be born again.

Pressing forward, our free will or agency is a gift from God. Throughout our lives, we must use that agency to set priorities and make good choices because some of our choices have led to pain and sorrow that have held us back temporarily from receiving our blessings. Some of our bad choices can be revisited. Good or bad choices can follow a person into adulthood. However, some of our bad choices can be rectified through Jesus Christ because He is the only one that can remove them permanently. There are always consequences for the bad choices we make. When we say yes to our soul in a positive sense, the enemy is kicked off balance, and we will live a victorious life. When we say no to our soul and follow our own path, it is more likely the soul will flood with worries and painful regrets. Sometimes this might cause an individual's healing and prosperity to be delayed.

God gives us neck-turning blessings that come in all types of packages. For instance, when you have overloaded yourself with bills and cannot see your way out, God turns that thing around for your good. God is able because what seems impossible to us is possible with God. That is why we cannot let the love of money get ahead of the love of God, nor allow greed to get ahead of God's purpose for our lives.

The truth is that many people have been blinded by the worldly system to make it to the top. They destroy others to make their dreams come to pass. The enemy plays a huge role in deception. As long as the enemy can keep you believing that you are your sole provider, then you have been locked in for a great fall.

This is where pride will set in, and the person can be identified with the nursery rhyme '*Humpty Dumpty*.' He "sat on the wall, and he had a great fall, and all the king's horses and all the king's men could not put Humpty together again." The comprehension of this rhyme in my mind, he was so proud of his own accomplishments until he did not give honor to God, who blessed him to acquire his wealth. When someone falls, it is going to be a great fall if they do not allow Christ to be the center of their accomplishments.

Allow me to close this chapter with an important reminder: do not let people, money, success, work, or any other vice prevent you from giving God that which is due unto Him if you desire a neckturning blessing.

CHAPTER SIX
Spiritual Visitations

In this chapter, I am going to share my experience with spiritual visitations. These spiritual moments cannot be fully captured in words, but I will attempt to share them to the best of my ability. I believe that these moments represent the immeasurable love that God has for His children. When you read this account, I hope that it strengthens your faith in God's love for you.

On April 8, 2012, at approximately 0200 hours Michigan Eastern Time at 0100 hours Alabama Central Time, I had a powerful out-of-body experience. My brother, Michael, telephoned me prior to this date to inform me that our sister, Pat, had taken a turn for the worse. She had gone into cardiac arrest. Allow me to backtrack for a few minutes to discuss her previous heart conditions. In 1971, she underwent heart surgery. It lasted thirtynine years. In 2010, the doctor recommended another heart surgery that was also successful.

A week after her second surgery, I flew SkyMiles to Detroit, Michigan, and spent a week or more assisting her back to health. She was literally making great progress toward recovery when I departed to return home to my husband, family, and professional occupation.

A year later, she had a heart attack and slipped into a coma. We were informed by the physicians that she would never come out of the coma; if so, she would not have any signs of consciousness. To put it bluntly, she would be in a persistent vegetative state, appearing to be awake but without awareness of her surroundings. Nevertheless, she came out of the coma and recognized her family and friends, but she had a long recovery.

So when Michael called to inform me of her condition, I was not surprised. Prior to Michael's call, I had already felt a coldness, a sickness, and an uneasiness in my spirit. Usually when I feel this way, something upsetting has occurred. At that moment, I knew she had passed this earthly life, but I was hoping it was not true and that the enemy was attacking my mind. However, I knew in my spirit this was not the enemy but an undesirable truth.

Permit me to discuss with you the spiritual moment that occurred through all of the hurt and pain that I was housing. I was lying on my couch when I sensed the presence of God. Immediately, I knew that He had come to me because my sister had passed. I asked the Lord, "Did she make it?" I politely interrupted the Lord when He addressed me as "Daughter." I said, "that is okay." I asked again, "Did she make it?" The Lord spoke again and said, "Daughter." I was not sure what He was going to say. I said, "that is okay." But I said it again, "Did my sister make it?" This exchange was repeated three times. The Lord knew my heart. He knew that I wanted to know. In a still, small voice, God whispered, "Yes."

My sister accepted Jesus but had issues with just giving her all and all to God. Of course, none of us are perfect, but we must continue to strive for perfection. We must constantly thank God for His grace and mercy because there is only one perfect person who has walked the face of this earth, and His name is Jesus Christ.

Continuing with the spiritual moment, I was like the apostle Paul in the Bible. I cannot say whether I was in-the-body or out-of-thebody. But I was standing face to face with my sister; however, I could not touch her, and she could not touch me. There was a shield between us. My sister spoke to me. I had not heard her voice for practically a year. She was loud and clear.

"Hey Teresia, I made it!" She had great enthusiasm in her voice. I could not see her body frame as it appeared in the flesh; it was more of a silhouette, but I knew it was her. Then, she began describing the beauty of heaven and its many levels. I observed a shining light.

I asked, "What is the shiny light?"

"God and Jesus," she said. The light was shining the brightest where God and Jesus were. There was a gust of activity in the background.

"What are they doing, Pat?"

She said, "The angels are on the second level, and people on the other levels are busy assembling things together. It is so peaceful here, and I am not in pain anymore!"

I saw a colossal of numbers shaped like doves flying into heaven. They were landing on different levels before God, Jesus, the Holy Spirit, and angels.

"What is the significance of the numbers?" I asked. She said, "it is the people's ages who are leaving earth and entering into heaven."

Then I asked, "Do you see my number?"

She answered, "I cannot really say; only God knows it, but there are all kinds of numbers. You were right about everything in the Bible, and heaven is definitely real! Do you remember the story about the rich man and Lazarus? Please tell everyone that it is true and to please give their lives to Christ Jesus if they have not."

I said, "Okay, I will."

Pat continued, "I wish you were here, but no! You have to wait for your own number. I must go; they are coming to show me around some more. You know, I just entered. See you later!" Whenever we departed, we would never say "bye." We would always say, "See you later."

I watched my sister's silhouette walk away with another bright light. When I snapped back to myself, I was in my living room on the couch. I arose and began to praise God, thanking Him that my sister had made it! I shared this experience in a testimony to my church.

I remained at home the rest of the day. I did not want to answer the phone, but it was impossible after family and friends heard about our great loss. After finally settling down at bedtime I begin to reminisce on the encounter that occurred between my sister and me. We were close because our mother passed when we were small children.

I could not shake the experience from my mind. I prayed and meditated on God's goodness and how He loved and blessed me to experience such a powerful encounter with my sister in her heavenly home. I asked the Lord later about this visit that I had with my sister. The only way that I can explain it to others is the way I received it from God. This was a spiritual out-of-body moment that captured a sacred, sudden, intense appearance in heaven that was orchestrated by God.

Jesus said, "In my Father's house, there are many mansions." I am striving to reside in one. I urge you to make sure your name is written in the Book of Life as well.

I am going to continue the path that God has placed me on because I am preparing to reside in paradise. I look forward one day to glimpse the Father and His Son in the position of authority on the first level in heaven.

Another occasion of a supernatural moment happened on a hot, scorching summer night. I was sitting in our vehicle waiting for my unsaved husband during that period of my life. He was pumping gas into the vehicle. I looked up, and over the florist shop, there was a cloud formed in the silhouette of a man. The Holy Spirit said one word, "Jesus," I watched the cloud move toward me. It seemed to disappear, and when I looked out of the passenger side of the vehicle's window, a man was standing there with a Glock weapon in his hand, staring at me as if he was contemplating whether he should blow my brains into pieces.

The Holy Spirit spoke to my spirit and informed me to look directly into the window of this man's soul-his eyes. He stood there a minute. Then he humbled himself as if he were looking at someone else in addition to me. He dropped his head and walked away as if he was ashamed. Later, I learned that this man was angry because, during that time my husband owed the furious man some money and was avoiding him. He recognized my husband at the gas station. I did not realize the man who was staring at me had already attacked my husband until later.

Afterward, I asked the Lord what happened at the gas station. It was days later before I received an answer, and it came through my pastor, the late Lucille Ritchie's sermon. She said, "Sometimes we will experience some dark places in our lives, but God will fight your battle if we only trust in Him. When we say yes to His will and go on to follow Him, He will cover you with His mercy and give you the victory every time."

Our God is an on-time God. Remember this: whether it is a pleasant or unpleasant situation, praising the Lord will produce good fruit in dangerous situations in a believer's life. We have some evil spiritual snipers who endeavor to take us out, but we must trust God's Word in the process because He said, "I will rebuke the devourer for your sakes, So that he will not destroy the fruit of your ground, Nor shall the vine fail to bear fruit for you in the field." I still cannot put all the pieces together related to the encounter at the gas station. I believe the silhouette of a man was Jesus. I also believe that He reached the conscience of the furious man, and he walked away in humiliation. I will always be grateful to the Lord. He is my protector, my strength, my fortress, and the one who will fight my expected and unexpected battles.

I have many more supernatural events that occurred that I can share with you, and I am sure you have some of your own supernatural moments with God as well. However, I am asking that you grace me with a little more of your time during your reading and grab your favorite beverage as you finish reading this chapter.

Two decades ago, my oldest daughter, Vernita, and I enjoyed a shut-in that we used to have at our former church. On the last night, between twelve and one o'clock in the wee hours of the morning, the late Bishop Ritchie wrapped everything up so that we could attend the service later that Sunday morning. After leaving that amazing service where the spirit consumed our spirits with love, peace, and joy, we were eager to share this experience with others about the goodness of Jesus.

We lived in a community where violent crimes were high. When we arrived at our apartment complex, many nights, we would have to park down the street in the parking lot and walk to our apartment. On this particular night there were no nearby parking spaces to our apartment. We had to park about half of a block from our apartment. As we were walking to our apartment complex, a man appeared from behind a tree and began walking directly toward us in a fast manner.

My daughter Vernita screamed, "Mama!" and I screamed, "Jesus!" The guy continued to charge towards us. Rape crimes were widespread during that era. We were too shocked to move, and as he came closer, there was a devilish look in his eyes. He stopped suddenly as if someone was standing in front of us. The devilish look on his face became a look of fear. He backed all the way across the street behind a tree and glanced for half of second in our direction. Then he started running in the opposite direction away from us. I sensed the presence of someone standing in front of me, but there was no human image to visualize. There was a calmness from my daughter and me. As we continued walking to our apartment, we began to praise God!

I believe at that present moment there were protective angels standing in front of us. The Bible tells us that angels are looking out for us. These types of supernatural moments will definitely bring you closer to God. This moment brought my daughter and me closer to Him.

I am not saying that we will not experience some dark moments in our lives. I am saying that God has our backs when we are faceto-face with deep troubles, such as a rapist or any other crime. God has a ram in the thicket for us. His Word says, "Weapons might form against us, but they cannot prosper."

I experienced another spiritual moment when my Auntie Fran, my father's sister, became extremely ill. She was diagnosed with liver cancer. Now, this spiritual moment I am sharing caused tremendous fear in me for a moment. My sister, Margaret, and I prayed and asked our auntie to accept Jesus Christ as her personal Lord and Savior. She was a fireball. However, she was a sweet lady in her own person. Auntie Fran was admitted to the hospital to be treated for her condition. I would visit her at the hospital and read the Bible to her. She became so unruly in the hospital that she had to be restrained to prevent her from pulling the tubes out of her nostrils and arms.

One day, my son, William, and I were visiting her. She became very unruly. As I stood over her praying, she sat up in the bed and looked me directly in my eyes. She only had one eye because she lost vision in one eye when she was eighteen years old. She said years ago that, an elderly lady told her to put an old remedy in her eye to clear up the pink eye. This remedy caused infection, and she became blind in her left eye.

I began to pray for total healing in her body. She rose up in the bed with a deep demonic voice and asked, "Why are you trying to save her soul?" She was restrained so that she did not harm herself or the hospital staff who were attending to her. It seemed like some type of demonic power had taken over her body. I was a newborn

Christian, and it scared me into a sweat! The nurse came in, and she witnessed the event that was occurring. When she heard this deep, loud, demonic voice coming from my Auntie Fran, she ran back out of the room to get the medical staff. My knees were knocking together, and I was about to faint when I heard the voice of the small, white Christian lady in Bed A. This lady had shared her belief in God with me prior to this incident. She shouted out, "Keep praying, baby!" "Do not stop!" For some reason, this activated God's power in me when I heard her shouting, "Keep praying." My faith in the Lord became stronger, and I called the demonic entity out; I screamed, "Go now, in the name of Jesus!" I continued to shout, "Jesus! Jesus! Jesus!" I kept saying, Jesus! Jesus! Jesus! My Auntie Fran fell back into the bed as if she was a ragdoll.

Later in my prayer time, of course, I want to know why God allowed me to experience something so fearful. I felt an empowered energy saturated my spirit, and a still small voice spoke to me and said, "The once greatest archangel Satan, who betrayed me, is real, and by no means take him for granted. But you have the key to defeat him through my Son. That is why you were able to use your God given power to cast the evil one out of your auntie." My Auntie Fran lived a few years after the hospital incident. She accepted the Lord as her personal Lord and Savior before she passed.

Lastly, this spiritual moment occurred at a Roll Tide Game. My children and I were late arriving, and there were no empty parking spaces. We had to park on the street in a neighborhood where crime was high. After the game, my oldest daughter Vernita, my son William, and my baby girl Tanesha were arguing about who was going to drive home. I had driven there, and I informed them that one of them must drive back. They had a big discussion about who was and who was not going to drive home. Sunset was slowly appearing; the time was ripe for criminal activities on the street to begin. We were still standing there debating who was going to surrender and drive home.

A tall, slim black man with a powerful energy exuding from his person and carrying a brown paper bag in his hand approached us. With a soft, vibrant voice, the man said, "It is not safe to stand here and debate." You all should get into your vehicle and leave now." He placed emphasis on NOW. Then he walked off and disappeared right before our eyes. We all quickly entered the vehicle, and I drove back home.

We were very quiet in the vehicle, pondering what we had just witnessed. We were thinking about how this man had appeared and disappeared in a split second. I can definitely say that angels are among us. They come to us in our darkest hours when trouble is all around us and provide a way to escape. Sometimes they reveal themselves, and sometimes they do not. When my daughter, Vernita, and I were about to be attacked in our neighborhood, I believe the attacker obviously saw an angel or angels, yet my daughter and I did not. However, I felt the presence of a warm and protective spirit. When we were contemplating a driver on the street, the angel revealed himself. I believe that the slim black gentleman who had some type of extraordinary energy flowing from his person was an angel. God always sends someone to grace us with His mercy in our time of need.

Thank you, Lord, for sending angels down from above. The Bible tells us to trust God, and He will always take good care of us." Please stay humble, stay prayerful, and stay faithful to God. He will increase your faith and reveal Himself unto you.

CHAPTER SEVEN
The Healing Power of God

Many people walk away from the opportunity to have a spiritual healing of the mind, body, and soul because they feel that it does not make sense. Authentic Christians can attest to the healing power of God. It takes one thing and one thing only, "believe." If you believe, then you will get what you need. Do you want to get well, or do you want to stay sick and feel hopeless that you will never get well?

There is a saying, "If you are always talking about what you do not have, then you will not have." I heard people say things like, "Let us be logical; this sickness is not going away." Of course, it is not going away if you constantly speak negatively in regard to your health. Here is the thing: God is so awesome and full of power. He created the body to heal itself over time. You cannot reason your situation away; you must have faith that God can do anything but fail. The Word of God informs us that faith is assurance, faith is hope, faith is evidence, and faith is the proof that God can and will heal you. Bring your mustard seed faith the next time the doctor tells you that you have a permanent disease.

Let me be clear on some things. There is nothing wrong with taking medications for the natural body because we have a body, soul, and spirit. The flesh needs some earthly medical assistance periodically. However, medications do not heal; medication only treats the symptoms. God gives man the ability in the medical field to assist with the treatment of the human body. If you take medications, do not stop taking your prescribed medications unless your doctor approves it. You must allow the medications to run their course. If you believe the Lord has imparted in your spirit to stop, make sure it is the Lord and not you. Conversely, if you are taking medications that are doing more harm than good, then you should speak to your physician about your concerns. Your physician may decide to change or discontinue the medication.

I cannot remember the day the Lord healed my knees, but it happened suddenly. I was working during that season when my knees were in excruciating pain. I could barely drive myself to work. When I arrived at work, I had to walk up a few steps to enter the building and my knees would be in unbearable pain.

However, I thanked the Lord every day for the healing of my knees. I remember the day when I arrived at work and a thought came to mind - walk up the handicap ramp because your knees are not going to get any better. I immediately recognized where that thought came from; I said, "My knees are healed in the name of Jesus." I continued to walk up those few steps, thanking the Lord all the way into the building, and one day, I realized that there was no physical sign of pain in my knees.

My knees were healed without taking any medication from the doctor or going to therapy. My healing has already been purchased and paid for by the blood of Jesus. So, are we coming to Him for something that has already been purchased? No! We are coming to Jesus to thank Him. Jesus said everything we need has already been paid for; it was purchased on Calvary. We must believe and speak the Word of God in every area of our lives.

In 2023, I experienced an alarming medical incident that caused me to collapse. My mustard seed faith rose to the occasion when I was diagnosed with an irregular heartbeat. The doctor was not sure if the cause was from certain medications that I was taking. He discontinued a certain type of high blood pressure medication because the medication can cause some people's heart rate to be extremely low. Also, if you are not drinking an adequate amount of water when taking certain medications, you may experience dehydration.

I became sick over the weekend and rushed to the ER, where I was admitted to the hospital. They explained to me that my heart had some abnormal activity, treated me for two days, and made an appointment to attend a vascular surgery center for further evaluation. The vascular surgery center team performed a nuclear test. The Lord showed me a vision of Himself sitting under a sycamore tree, holding my hospital chart. He spoke to me and said. "The tests will come back normal." The tests came back normal just as He assured me. However, the vascular doctor was not satisfied and placed a sensor and monitor on me for a month.

The Lord showed me a vision of standing under a maple tree and spoke to me and said, "Your God does not partially heal sickness. My children receive total healing." The Lord came the last and final time of this incident and showed me a fir tree and said, "Be patient and relax during the process because the result is normal." I was taught by my late pastors, Donald and Lucille Ritchie, not to wait until the battle is over, shout the victory now! I shouted the victory before the result was finalized.

There is no disease that exists in this world that Jesus cannot heal. But remember, He does it in His timing, and it is always right on time. I know it sounds a little condescending, but believe me, it is true. If Jesus is your Lord and Savior, and your faith is mixed with the Word of God, then the impossible becomes possible.

Let me attempt to explain the significance of the three trees that the Lord revealed to me. The sycamore tree represents its true stature, which is the tree of life. The maple tree pours out all the sweetness of the precious grace of God. The fir tree represents the determination and endurance that comes with hope. The Lord showed me these three visions to support my belief that His Word is true. I said all of that to say this: He can turn any negative situation into a positive outcome.

In another incident, I received an instant healing from the Lord. When God heals, it can be either instant or gradual. Sometimes, it is instant, and sometimes, it is a process of following instructions. However, He will heal in His set time, and it will be right on time.

I noticed a growth under my chin, and it began to grow larger. Three days later, it was the size of a small plum. I made a medical appointment to have the growth diagnosed. During my medical visit, the doctor informed me that he was not sure what type of growth it was. He explained that he did not feel comfortable giving me any type of medication. So, an appointment was scheduled with a specialist to diagnose my situation. I returned home and cried aloud. I said, "Whatever this is that has attached itself under my chin, I command it in the name of Jesus to disappear immediately." Afterward, I walked around all-day, thanking God for my healing. Amazingly, the next morning, the growth had disappeared.

I called the medical doctor and informed him that the growth had disappeared. He advised me to return to his office immediately. I arrived at the doctor's office and was escorted to an exam room. He rushed into the room to check the area and was amazed that the growth had definitely disappeared. The only logical answer he could provide was that sometimes a swollen gland can dissolve without treatment. Nevertheless, he pointed out that the growth was excessively large to dissolve overnight. He requested more tests, but I declined. I have not experienced any more problems with growth under my chin.

The Bible tells us plainly to trust in the Lord with all our heart and lean not to our own understanding. In all our ways, acknowledge Him, and He shall direct our paths.

We must put total faith in God and stop trying to reason things out. We must trust God in the process and believe that we are healed by His stripes. When we totally believe, we will totally receive.

Some people receive their healing through other people's faith prayers. But God healed them. The person did not heal the individual. The Word of God tells us that prayer and faith of the elders will save the sick, but the Lord is the one who raises them up, not the elders. In other words, someone else's faith prayers can cause you to receive your healing, but it is your faith that will retain your healing. God does the healing, but we must initiate strong faith through the Word of God to receive and retain healing.

Numerous people proclaim healing hands. Let me say this: always get permission from the person, a family member, or a person in authority before laying hands on a sick person. When laying hands on individuals, tell them to be healed in the name of Jesus. There is no other name that we might be saved or healed. Many are true men and women of God, and some are counterfeits. Some are duplicates of real, genuine men and women of God. They desire the anointing yet lack faith. They are functioning without the power of God; therefore, people are being deceived. We have real men and women of God as well as counterfeits. Always remember that human beings cannot heal. God does the healing. Sincere men and women pray to God for your healing because they know that healing belongs to God's people. They also acknowledge that healing power comes from God.

God is so profound that He allows an individual to endure sickness for years without healing them. Think about this: Paul endured a throne in his flesh, meaning he had some type of pain that God did not remove. But it did not hinder Paul from doing the work of the Lord. If you are sick and want to be healed, ask God to heal you and walk in faith. However, continue to follow the physician's orders and wait patiently on the Lord; He will heal you in His set time and it will be right on time.

CHAPTER EIGHT
Our Fight is Spiritual

I have heard it said that "anybody can fight," but the onehundred-dollar question is: "Did you win?" As a student in elementary, junior high, and high school, there were many fights. Every student wanted to know, "Did you win?" I seldom engaged in physical fights when I was growing up, but I never let anyone push me around or attack me without defending myself.

I never wanted to be known as a baddy because that is nothing more than a bully, and most people do not like bullies. I definitely do not like bullies. I have seen people despise a person known as a baddy yet tolerate an individual's behavior to obtain something from that person. In many cases, some people will lie or place a baddy at a scene where they were absent just to get them into trouble with peers, parents, and sometime with law enforcement.

Everything in the natural world has significance in the spiritual realm. When fighting an opponent in a natural way, people will give their all to defend themselves. Many Christians exercise their faith in God's Word, which tells them they do not have to fight their battles because the Lord fights them. In the Bible, the Word of God says, "Vengeance is mines; I will repay." God will surely fight our natural and spiritual battles.

The Word of God assures us that we should not stay angry or take matters into our own hands when something overwhelming or disappointing occurs. Notice, I said *stay angry* because the Bible tells us to "Be ye angry and sin not." We are emotional beings, and at some point, we are going to experience anger. But we must regroup and let it dissolve if we want to be continually blessed.

Have you heard the saying "Fight or flight." When a person is a bully, the person being bullied would rather take flight than fight.

We have to train ourselves to stand up against bullies who are influenced by demons in the spiritual realm. We have to win the battle by using the Word of God when demonic spirits come against the human flesh through another human being. Our defense is the Word of God, and we must have our war garments on as a shield against our opponent. We must protect ourselves and our families against dark spirits on a daily basis. The enemy is real in this world. If you do not believe that the enemy is real, then you are not prepared for the battle.

I plead with you today to accept the Lord who died for you so that you may have life because, without Him, you are in a state of hopelessness. If you do not accept God's son, then the enemy has accomplished his mission in your life.

There is a difference between Satan and Jesus. Satan is sneaky and deceitful. Jesus is truth and all powerful. Let us travel back in the scripture for a moment and notice how David received the victory over Goliath. Goliath was a strong warrior and huge in size. However, God gave David the victory with one shot from his sling that landed in the center of Goliath's forehead.

Peter stated that "Satan is like a roaring lion." One word that Peter used changed the trajectory of Satan: the word *like*. It indicates similarity, but the comparison is not the same. The enemy tries to compare himself to a strong lion that has powerful strength to make us afraid.

The enemy is a real evil spirit roaring around, attacking those who are weak and vulnerable. His main goal is to drive a wedge between God's people and God. If he can succeed, the shining light you have will become dim. His goal is to prevent others from distinguishing the difference between God's people and the world. When the enemy controls Christians through his trickery devices, they have reached a stage where they are just repeating the letter of God's Word with no power. The enemy will have you thinking that your light is shining, but in reality, your light is dim, and the Holy

Spirit has shut down to a deactivated stage. At this point, you need to run for your life and call on Jesus to renew your strength and restore you to your rightful place in Him.

Again, we do not have to fight our battle because our battle is the Lord's. I mentioned these very words to a close relative of mine. This individual was incredibly angry with the devil. He felt the enemy was continually taking his belongings from his property and stated that "the devil must die." I explained to him how the enemy works and that the devil is a spirit and cannot be killed with natural weapons. However, we can rebuke and cast demonic spirits out of the human flesh.

We cannot pretend to have godly power; we must have God's special working power. The only way to obtain this power is to have a relationship with Jesus. If not, you might find yourself running out of the house seeking support from someone that truly has the power of God when being attacked by the enemy. Remember in Chapter Six, *Spiritual Visitations*. When a demon possessed my Auntie Fran, I was trying to rebuke the demon or demons as a newborn Christian. I described a Christian lady in Bed A who encouraged me to keep praying. I almost lost it, and if she had not been present, I believe I would have run out of the room like the seven sons of Sceva. I was beginning to doubt the effectiveness of my prayer because of the extremely strong demonic effect that was present in the room. But thank God that He always has a ram in the bush. The angel stopped the demon or demons through encouragement from the lady in Bed A. She was crying aloud, and this helped me to regain strength to continue the prayer. As Christians, we must believe that God will always have a way out for His Children.

We must also remember that the devil tempts us with all kinds of sinful acts. The top three are money, entanglement, and temptation. We must soak ourselves in God's Word and follow His instructions for our lives. If not, Satan is certainly going to offer counterfeit happiness. God's plans protect our hearts to fight off the temptation when the devil tempts us. Whenever we encounter temptations, we must fight back with our faith in God. When our faith is dipped in the Word of God and fed daily, we access oneness with God, which produces peace within us.

Also, we have to denounce any worry that the enemy attempts to cloud our minds and hearts with because worry robs us of our peace. We must let God's Word remove any worry that attempts to attach itself to our minds and hearts. Always fight the enemy with the Word of God. Remember, the battlefield of our mind is the primary place where spiritual warfare begins. This is where the enemy fights for strongholds to blind us to our blessings. We must submit ourselves to God and resist the devil in any form that he might appear. Most importantly, dispose of any thoughts that do not line up with God's Word, and the enemy will flee from you. God's Word is true. I have been tempted on many occasions by Satan's devices, but I received victory through the Word of God.

The enemy will continue to find any type of loophole that is open, but always be ready to give him a black eye with the Word of God. Sometimes, it seems that you are fighting the battle all alone, but God will settle the score with the enemy in His set time. Remember, God's set time will always be right on time. If you choose to fight, fight spiritually and not naturally. Therefore, you will always win the battle with the Lord!

CHAPTER NINE
Keep Moving In Christ

An individual inner man will always have the passion of the Lord through the Holy Spirit. A person must always keep moving in the direction that the Spirit of God is leading him or her. Do not sit still unless the Lord has spoken directly to you. When God instructs you to sit still, then stay there until He encourages your spirit to go forth. I do not have to ask God what He wants me to do for this dying world because I know He called all blood washed believers to present the gospel. God has already given us permission to go forth to present the gospel through His Word. However, we must follow the guidelines that pertain to His Word.

The world has so many crazy challenges today. This is why we must have that quiet assurance in Jesus. We will be alright as long as Jesus abides within us. We will be safe, we will have joy, and we will have everlasting peace. Many times, we have missed the mark of God's plan. The reason we missed the mark is because we are not perfect. But missing the mark should not be the norm for a Christian. I strive to keep moving until the Holy Spirit reveals the right plan. Do not sit for years asking God repeatedly what He will have you do or waiting for God to reveal His plan.

Sometimes, God puts us in difficult situations to keep us from becoming comfortable and even conceited. There is nothing wrong with having self-love, but it must be balanced. Some people think only of themselves. God precisely instructs us not to let pride overtake us. It is very necessary that you keep moving because any direction without sinning is suitable. If you keep moving, God will reveal to you - through the Holy Spirit – if the direction in which you are moving is the right direction.

God will open the doors designed specifically for you and close the ones that will harm you. Just trust God in the process. When

God speaks, listen to the still, small voice because it will never fail you. If you have God's salvation and His power, then you are anointed with His favor. So arise and start moving in the direction God has mapped out for you.

When you give your life to Christ, you must have assurance the Lord will make everything alright. Just give Him what is due, which is to give Him praise. This is especially important when you are placed in an uncomfortable or unsafe environment. I often think about the little boy who was abducted and refused to stop singing. The news anchor said the child kept singing, "Every praise unto my God, every word of worship with one accord, every praise, every praise, every praise is to our God." The abductor told the child to stop singing that song. The little boy would not stop singing, and the kidnapper finally released the child.

The enemy cannot cope with the praises of God. When praises go up, blessings come down. You do not have to speak vocally all the time or do a praise dance. Speak to God just like He speaks to you - in a still, small voice. You can give Him praise without shouting to the top of the mountain because the Bible does not indicate that God has a hearing problem.

Nevertheless, it matters not how you decide to praise Him; just give Him what is due to Him because He is worthy of all the glory, all the praise, and all the honor. He is Jehovah Elyon, which expresses the extreme sovereignty and majesty of God and His highest preeminence. He has all the power and authority in the universe.

Some people think there should be a place and time to praise the Lord. Not so! God inhabits the praises of His people anywhere and anytime. Again, it does not have to be outward. We have an inward spirit to praise God as well. However, some people are more outward in praise than others. The Word of God tells us to rejoice always, pray continually, and give thanks in all circumstances because this is the will of God for those who are in Christ.

If you feel embarrassed about giving God some praise for His goodness in front of others, let me ask you this question: Do you have a problem with God blessing you in front of others? Of course not! I am not going to allow people to stop me from giving honor to whom honor is due.

When you receive joy on the inside and desire to express it from the outside, then go for it. It is your choice, Inward or outward; just keep the Holy Ghost activated. Do not let the Holy Spirit lie dormant because if you do not exercise it regularly, the enemy has the opportunity to keep you in bondage. Keep the Holy Spirit; stir the flame so that His power remains implanted within your heart. Just remember, no matter what the circumstances look like - you must keep praising the Lord.

The little child kept moving in faith in Jesus by sending praises up in song to the Lord when he was in a dangerous situation. He received his joy from the inner voice of God within himself because this is where the peace of God abides.

Moving forward, there is a story in the Bible where this servant was given one talent by his lord, and he went and buried it. When his lord returned, he wanted to know if the man received a profit from the talent. The servant said, "I knew you were a hard man, so I decided to bury it." This man was demanded by his lord to dig up his talent and give it to the servant who had doubled his five talents to ten talents. This servant had invested his talents and received a profit.

I strongly urge you not to bury your talent by standing still; use your talent to bless others. We must have the determination to work and use the talent that God gives us. If I am honest with myself and the person reading this, at first, I was reluctant to work on my talents because I felt unworthy and afraid.

Nevertheless, I worked on my talents because I realized that it was more favorable for me to work on my God-given talents and gifts and not let the enemy control my thoughts or keep me bound. This is what happened to my birth father, which I discussed in Chapter Three, *God Orchestrate Lives.*

It would not be wise to tell God to use you just to be accepted by people or to have a super platform for admiration. I encourage you not to run from the plan that you know God has assigned to you. But keep moving in the direction in which He is leading you. It is not only for you but for others who will reap the benefit from your courage to accomplish their assignments as well. It is important that you work toward completing your assignments because your blessings are attached to the assignments.

I have heard some people say, "It is not time for me to die because I have not finished my assignments." God will let you know when you come to the end of your race, even if the job has not been completed. However, you would have finished your portion when you physically die.

Moses was working on his assignments until God explained to him that he would not go into the Promised Land. Then God assigned Joshua to continue the assignment. The only time a person needs to sit still is when God commands it. I urge you not to sit still because, after a while, it might become the norm for you.

Sometimes, God allows or even arranges difficulties in our lives. During these difficult times, we grow in faith and develop more of the characteristics of His son. Tests and trials can reveal what we really believe inside our hearts. Sometimes, we can be tempted to take matters into our own hands. Have you ever thought to yourself or even said out loud, "I am not going to put up with this mess anymore!" Well, I have. But when this occurs, I remember to do what I said in Chapter Four, *P.O.T Experiences.* In order to receive the victory, I have the three second rules: Stop, Drop, and Roll. This indicates that you are giving your frustration and problem to God because when we take matters into our own hands, we are delaying our blessings.

If you are not sure God is telling you to wait or to keep moving, then turn your attention to the four lepers in the Bible. They said, "If we sit here, we are going to die. If we go inside, the soldiers might kill us, but one thing is for sure: if we sit here, we are surely going to die."

What do you think you should do? Do you need to sit or move? When I was in a similar situation, such as the four lepers. I imitated the four lepers. I did not sit idly around waiting for something to occur; I did what I thought was best for me. However, I screamed out, "Lord, if I am on the wrong boat, stop this boat now!" Because I want to be on the boat that Jesus is on.

Another positive thing you can do is to pay attention to the ranges in your life because I have observed things in my life shift within my range and sometime out of range. When they are within range, I keep moving, and when they are out of range, I respectfully wait patiently for the Holy Spirit to guide me accordingly.

There is an acquaintance of mine who sat around all day waiting for the Spirit to speak and has not taken the initiative to do anything. If you have the Holy Spirit living inside of you, He will speak. When He does, I encourage you to start moving in the direction of the plan that has already been mapped out for you. The Lord will definitely open up doors that will help you and close doors that are of no avail.

We must remember that trials are designed to test us. Often, we do not address an issue until we are in a situation where we have no choice. We need to face the issue by asking the One who created us to guide us in the right direction according to the situation that is at hand. He will move for us in His set time, and it will be right on time. It is God's will for us to stay in peace and make decisions with godly wisdom in every circumstance in our lives. However, when you are faced with a test or trial and waiting for your deliverance, let the joy of the Lord reign within you, and it will manifest itself on the outside in the presence of others.

We have many temptations in this world, especially during right and wrong decision making. Sometimes, Christians can be tempted to go back to old habits. The enemy will give assignments to his demons to tempt you in many ways. For instance, if you were delivered from drugs, the demons will tempt you by using a family member, a friend, or others to entice you to start an old drug habit that was previously broken. Now, here is where the choice comes in for you. You can omit or submit to God. If you make the choice to omit God's order, then the devil will fulfill your desires that will ultimately destroy you. However, when we surrender ourselves to God, then it is easier for us to trust Him to deliver us from our bad habits. He will give us the strength to resist the devil's temptation and receive victory.

Once God delivers, you do not entertain the devil's proposals anymore. You might have to separate yourself from those individuals who are enticing you to open those once closed doors. I advise you to move according to the will of God. Sometimes, God delivers people, and they sit around with that same mentality as if they have never been delivered because they are still entertaining those unhealthy habits.

Satan will tempt individuals and give them excuses as to why they should fulfill their desires. He will torment your mind over and over. Sometimes, Satan wins because the person's weakness for this particular thing over-power their ability to rebuke him. Satan's devices are extremely dangerous; therefore, it is important for your soul to submit humbly to God. If you have not accepted Christ as Lord and Savior, the devil will make you an offer. If you accept it, you are putting your soul in jeopardy. If you die a physical death in that stage, it will be God's decision where your soul will abide. I urge you not to sign the devil's contract; it will be more profitable to accept God's covenant.

God has a great plan for our lives, and we must trust that He is in control. He will work things out for our good when we are going through various temptations. You must inform the enemy that he is powerless against the miraculous power of God.

On the other hand, if this test is from God, I assure you that you will grow closer to God as you go through it. You will thank Him for this test. I know it sounds trivial to thank the Lord that your body is racked with pain, or your spouse walked out of the marriage, or your child is on drugs. However, you will realize in time that this test made you stronger and more like Christ.

Faith is the key to our victory because faith is the assurance of things hoped for and the conviction of things not seen. We cannot see faith just like we cannot see air, but we know that it is there.

Sometimes, we pray for something God has already given us. In most cases, the person is either afraid, lazy or simply procrastinates to work the plan. Being afraid is in the arena of people pleasers. A person who is a people-pleaser worries about others' opinions, responses, and acceptance. Our first priority should be, is God satisfied with how we handled the situation and not how people say it should have been handled. People do not have the power of life and death in their hands.

Laziness is in the arena of self-pleaser. Some people lack confidence in themselves, or they develop an unhealthy lifestyle because the body wants to constantly enjoy pleasure. There is nothing wrong with a body experiencing pleasure as long as it is not sinful or harmful to self or others. Nevertheless, if these things take priority over the things of God, then you are a self-pleaser. You must make a conscious decision to follow after the things that are of God. "Seek the Kingdom of God and His righteousness, and all these things will be added unto you," said the Lord.

Procrastination is part of the family of laziness and fear; however, it stands alone because it is self-harm. You actually avoid the assignment that God has given you because you are not sure you can handle the task, or you think you are going to mess it up.

Now, you become frustrated and angry because of the doubt. Remember this: if God provided you with the assignment, your response to the task is to accept it. Keep moving in the direction that God has mapped out for you.

62

CHAPTER TEN
All-In

A natural scenario of an all-in is when you have a favorite team; perhaps it is a football, basketball, or some other sport. You think your favorite basketball team is the bomb no matter who that team plays, whether they win or lose, you are a diehard. You are all-in because you believe in the team, you support the team, you are a fanatic, and you are there for the long haul. In other words, you are rolling with them in victory or defeat. You are all-in, no matter what.

This should be the same mindset when it comes to walking with the Lord. We must be all-in because He made it crystal clear in His word, "If any man will come after me, let him deny himself, and take up his cross, and follow Me." Following Him gives you access to eternal life because God's son went all-in for us when He died on Calvary. Jesus gave His life for us, so we have the choice to give our lives to Him. The point is clear-cut: we cannot go all-in if we are exhibiting resistance to the Word of God.

Resistance to God's way is doing little ungodly things that you think are unnoticeable. You must give your own heart permission to show you little ungodly things that you think are unnoticeable. If you are still in denial of your action, then you have chosen not to go all in. We usually ignore it when the spirit shows us ourselves by saying things like, "Nobody is perfect, or do not judge me." Have you met or know a person who always justifies what they do? Never in a million years do they say, "I was wrong; I made a mistake; I am sorry, etc." These types of people are a walking time bomb for disaster because they do not take any accountability for their actions. But most of all, they are unfaithful to the Lord. So, there is no earthly way they are going to be faithful to anybody. Their longevity to faithfulness is transient.

Unlike Jesus, we do not live perfect lives. We definitely make mistakes, but we must own them and continue on the wheel of eternal progress. This propels us into movement and advancement toward constantly doing our best to be faithful to God, self, and others. I know we are saved by grace, and this means that God forgives us of all of our sins. But here is the thing: repentance is available to us; it allows us to improve by endeavoring to do our very best in every area of our lives. It is not profitable for you to do evil deeds and walk away as though you are untouchable.

Admit your faults to the Lord because it redefines you, and this allows you to create an opportunity for building a strong relationship between God and you and other people. When you tell a person that you are sorry, it really does not affect them. They may appreciate you for admitting your fault because admitting your fault will get you back into the right fellowship with God, and maybe the person you offended will accept your apology. The main thing is that you will have peace within.

Our free will is a gift from God, throughout our walk in the earth, we must use it to set priorities and make good choices. Some bad choices that we make might lead to pain and sorrow that hold us back from becoming more like our heavenly Father. To be all-in, we must make good choices on this earth. Although God gives us free will to choose, there are consequences for the bad choices we make.

Let me share a true story with you. A young lady with a college degree married a young man who did not attend college. He was a sanitation employee. They were happily married, but the young lady's mother was constantly advising her that she could do better. The mother was manipulated by the enemy without being aware of it. Of course, any mother wants the best for their child, but this mother should have sought God in her ambitions. The mother convinced her daughter that she needed a marriage partner with a college degree as well. This young lady listened to her mother's advice, and when she met a college educator, she divorced her faithful husband and married the college educator. In less than a year, the new husband - who was a college educator - killed her. This is why it is crucial to seek God in everything and not man. Man will fail you, although, most of the time, it is not intentional. I am sure her mother meant well, but the enemy set the young lady up using her mother as bait to destroy her. Even when it comes to our closest relatives whom we believe have our best interest at heart, we must still take our concerns to the One who created us because He will never fail us.

Moving forward, we must stop praying prayers of unbelief. In my opinion, unbelief prayers are when an individual prays and does not believe God is going to answer the prayer. They have already accepted in their heart this prayer is not going to come to pass. It is essential that we pray prayers in faith. This means we are praying with the intention and belief that He will answer our prayers. Faith prayers get an on-time answer from an on-time God because He responds to the heart, not just the words. It is important, when we pray, to pray from the heart in faith.

Let us stop living loosely on the enemy's territory and live closely on the Holy Word of God and pray those full of faith, passionate prayers. Sincere prayers touch God's heart because emotions are attached to them to get exactly what we pray for. So therefore, make the right choices in life because if you have been transformed through the Word of God, then you are expected to live a holy lifestyle. For instance, there was this young guy, whose name I will omit to protect privacy. He surrendered his life to Jesus, and his entire family strived to live the lifestyle of a Christian. They were enjoying life to the fullest of Christ. Consequently, his friends started calling and sending him emails. As if that was not enough, they started messaging him on Facebook and Instagram, relating that they missed their smoking and drinking partner. Instead of this young man ignoring them, by closing the apps, not responding back, and continually studying the Word that would transform him from a carnally minded person to a spiritually minded person, he engaged in these ungodly conversations. Eventually, the old man was resurrected because he was not all-in anymore. They pulled on him until he became weary of well-doing and converted to a backslider. When you are all-in, you must denounce the old man and embrace the new man in Christ. As I said earlier, you will have to surround yourself with people who are going to build you up and not tear you down.

When you are not in Christ, you are working in your own strength, which is going to cause you to collapse. It will be profitable for you to read Chapter Two, *"Born A Sinner,"* and follow the prerequisite to becoming a Christian. When we are allin, God orchestrates our lives because He vowed to fulfill our every desire as we walk according to His Word. God is all-in for us, and He wants us to be all-in for Him.

When we are all-in, we must be willing to trust God to pass our tests in order to receive our neck turning blessings. Blessings come from the word *bless* and *bless* is a joyful state of those who find their purpose and fulfillment in God. Let me elaborate on what blessings are. Blessings are God's favor and protection, His mercy, and benefit. This is a miracle knowing it comes straight from God, even if sometimes it comes through people.

We can keep ourselves trapped from receiving our blessings by speaking negatively about our situation. I will never forget when I visited Fresh Anointing House of Worship, located on Virginia Loop Road. A jazz Christian artist was there to play Christian jazz. He used role-play to give us an example of how we can slow our own blessings down. He sat in the front of a line to role-play God. In the midst of the role-play, he put three of the people traveling with him in the line. The people were standing in line, waiting for their chance to be blessed. One of the ladies was placed in the line to put emphasis on jealousy. The other two ladies were supposed to be a cousin and a friend who were in the line to receive their blessings from the Lord.

Ms. Jealousy demeaned the ladies' characters. She first began with her cousin, stating, "How did she get in front of me, as much as I attend church? She only comes once a year, and she has received a new vehicle." The next lady was her friend, and when she approached God to receive a new home, Ms. Jealousy stated, "How did she get a new home before me? She is out all-night drinking and partying." When it was time for Ms. Jealousy to be blessed, the Lord sent her to the back of the line and it was a very long line. He sent her back because jealousy is a sin. Do you want to go to the back of the line? If you are demeaning people because you are jealous of their blessings, then ask God to remove them and make a conscious decision not to resurrect them because the choices we make can either hurt or bless us.

God does not base our salvation on our conduct, but we will reap what we sow because there are consequences for our actions. God sent the jealous young lady to the end of the line because she slowed her blessing down by talking negatively about others. You must understand that when we speak negatively, our hearts will condemn us. God will send us to the back of the line if we become jealous of another person's blessings.

The key point of the story is that jealousy is a strong, destructive emotion that can lead to sin. When it creeps into your heart, it can destroy you because God searches the heart of a person, and the person will receive their blessing according to their own heart. We can be trapped with the words of our own mouths and hearts. There is a saying, "If you do not have anything good to say about someone, do not say anything at all."

God will visit our conduct and will correct us. He chastens those whom He loves. God wants us to love one another and edify one another. When we are mistreated by someone we love, we must pray for them and let God handle it. I know it is not easy, but this is where denying self-emotions and placing your total trust in God can bring in a harvest of neck-turning blessings.

The worst thing I have ever witnessed is when I observe people speaking negatively about their own lives. I am not making light of a person's situation by any means. I know when it hits home, you want to know where you can kindle up some faith and strength. Sometimes, things happen extremely fast, and you can be totally devastated. However, to speak curses over your own life, such as, "I am no good; that is why I never have nothing." " I have no friends." Instead of speaking negatively about your situation, speak positively. Boldly state, "I am the child of a royal priesthood. I am blessed in every area of my life, and I am the head and not the tail." Do not give the enemy an opening into your life to destroy you. As far as friends, I once heard, " If you want a friend, you must show yourself to be friendly."

We must have faith in God because the very elite and the poorest of the poorest will throw you under the bus just to let themselves shine. Trust in the Lord with all your heart because God will always reveal Himself to you when you are all-in. I am eternally grateful for spiritual guidance and abundance of blessings through God's Word.

Whenever the enemy fights for a seat at your table, you must crush him quickly with the Word of God. The table that God has prepared for us in the presence of our enemy is ours and ours only. To be all-in, we must stand on God's Word and put all our confidence in the Lord by making God our first point of reference.

We must stay all-in because God knows what He is doing. He has it all planned out for His children. He has a plan to take care of us, not abandon us, and a plan to give us a future. God knows us because He created us, and He has already planned our future before the beginning of time. He knows all the rewards that He has for each of us. To be all-in, we must follow the will of God for our lives. We must love deeply, pray hard, think clearly, listen well, plan wisely, stand firmly, be attentive, and keep moving in Him.

To be all-in, we must follow God's direction, not our own direction because it is not in a person to direct him or her own path. Make sure He knows that you are all-in by accepting His son as your personal savior. God has blessings stored up for each of us; we just need to be on the receiving end to accept them.

If you have not started speaking blessings over your situations, such as, I am blessed, I am favored, I am smart, I am healthy and wealthy, start today. My motto is "I am Topfavor, which is God's favor." We must believe what we are saying. A well-known pastor shared his experience with all types of difficulties when he was trying to get a particular job. He explained that he kept crying out to God, and every time the enemy tried to plant in his mind, 'no way you are going to get this job,' he continued to cast down the vile statement of the deceiver. He spoke God's Word over his situation and believed that the position was his. The Word says, "Believe and you will receive. This pastor's faith, God's Word, and persistence caused him to receive the position. We cannot change things in the past that happened to us whether we brought it on ourselves or not. He said that he applied for a position similar to the position with another company and was not chosen. God has ordained specific blessings to occur in His set time, and it is right on time.

We must look to the future and thank God for Jesus because He is our advocate who stands in the gap for us. We can bless our present and our future by saying good, true, and godly words over situations that occur in our lives. We must maintain a good reputation and have a good conversation so that when we interact with others, they know that we are true, authentic people of God.

We must treat everyone with the same respect that we crave. My daddy would always emphasize treat everyone the way you would like to be treated because when you are on your sick bed, you do not know who might have to give you a glass of water. When a person becomes sick or loses a loved one, and you are angry prior to their dilemma, you must squash your anger and be there to support them in their time of need.

When we are angry and say something negative about another individual, we give life to it. If you are saying something negative about another person's situation, the moment you speak those words out of your mouth, you are allowing those words to take root. We do not realize that we just planted a bad seed in that person's life. We should always speak positive affirmations instead of negative condemnations.

Here is the key: we must send our words out in the direction to bless someone. Not only do we have to speak it, but we must believe it. Speak victory and abundance over a person's life. Then, you can receive the same blessings. We will produce what we say with our words. When we speak negatively about others or ourselves, this could be death or life because it is in the power of the tongue.

The word of God tells us, "Whosoever keepeth his mouth and his tongue, keepeth his soul from trouble." Sometimes, we need to stop talking constantly and listen to what the spirit is saying to us. Many times, we kill our own dreams because we are talking too much. Let us discipline ourselves by slowing down and listening because when we are talking, we are talking about information that is familiar. But when we are listening, most of the time, we learn something that we have no prior knowledge of.

There have been many times that I thought of something negatively and practically said it. However, I stopped myself from damaging my present and future. Some people speak too much nonsense about their marriage, about their children and family. Stop speaking that rubbish over your family. When negative thoughts come into our minds, it is to draw our attention away from

God. Then, we begin to engage in the enemy's territory, where, eventually, there will be heartaches, pain, and sorrow. At this point, you must use your creative power by casting negative thoughts quickly from your mind, and please do not verbalize them. Serve the enemy notice that you are not going to destroy your future by speaking negatively about your situation.

I am convinced if we cast down negative thoughts as soon as they have been hashed out in our hearts, they will not have time to take root. Have you ever had a crazy thought enter your mind, and you said to yourself, "Where did that come from?" The enemy planted it and wanted you to speak it because he knows the damage it would bring to you or someone close to you. We must be very careful because the enemy will use a familiar person to manipulate us to steal our joy.

Also, if the enemy can get you to become suspicious of those who really love you, then you will not have anyone to support you. You will be standing alone in whatever you strive to accomplish. Ask God to deliver you the thoughts that haunt you on a daily basis.

We must desire a good reputation and good standing with others. Most Christians are good, hearty people of God. For instance, my forever family members are Freedom Life Ministries, even though many have moved on. Some have started their own ministries. We were taught the Word of God by the late Bishop Donald Ritchie and late Pastor Lucille Ritchie. We accepted Christ and allowed the Holy Spirit to be activated and His power to flow through us. It brought about the love of God in us to speak favor into our lives and trust the Holy Spirit for guidance. The late Bishop and Pastor Lucille Ritchie are definitely responsible for our close-knitted Christian family, current and former members of Freedom Life Ministries to this very day. We might not always be in each other's company and sometimes disagree on certain topics. But when something pleasant or unpleasant occurs, we will be there to support each other.

We must be all-in, no matter what the circumstances look like. The enemy's job is to run to the scene in our minds when we are not thinking logically, when we are at our weakest, or when we are having trouble on every side. His goal is to destroy our hope and future.

Moreover, when it comes to materialistic things like a car or house, a child of God should not cry for a whole year about a repo or a house that was foreclosed five years ago. Stop! This is definitely not normal. We must let go and let God. You might be in a difficult time right now but let me challenge you. Do not use your words to describe the situation. Use God's Word to change the situation. Talk about the victory and not the defeat. When we are constantly quoting God's favor over our lives, we have just blessed favor into our present and future.

When you pray and believe God for what you have prayed for, one day, it will become a reality. Many years ago, a group of church women from Freedom Life Ministries started a single prayer breakfast led by a sweet sister-in-the Lord named Gloria. We prayed for many desired blessings from the Lord within the group.

A few of the single women prayed that God would bless them with a godly husband. He actually blessed those who really desired a godly husband. It was not instant for some of us, but the more we prayed and thanked Him, God honored our prayers. The majority of us are happily married today. For those who have not received their answer, they will in His set time, and it will be right on time. Many times, we say we are waiting on God. Actually, God is waiting for us to get real with Him because He has already ordained our blessings. We just need to spark our faith to receive it.

We must always talk about the solution to our problems, which is His Word. He will give us the desires of our hearts. If you are sick, let the weak say. "I am strong." You do not have to tell somebody else you are strong. Talk to yourself! Say, "Self, I am strong; my family is healed."

We must be all-in to position ourselves when God bombards us with His blessings. He is not a man that He shall lie. We must have the heart to bless others when God blesses us. We cannot be like the man in the Bible who had plenteousness and tore down his barns to build bigger ones in which to store his abundance. Yet, he did not share any of his blessings with others. We cannot just fix up the outside of our temple, the inside must be dressed up also because this is where the Spirit of God abides. We can look nice and sanctified, appearing holy from the outside while living selfrighteously on the inside.

Sharing your cares and concerns with a person is a great way to bond with them. But be careful who you constantly reveal your innermost thoughts, concerns, and joy with because the enemy will use that against you. I have seen a person who was in the world involved in some criminal activities. God saved and forgave the person, yet some people still observe that person as a criminal. That is why it is not a good idea to testify about your entire life. A person must only testify when God has given their heart permission to do so.

Confide your thoughts and concerns to Christ. Then, ask the Holy Spirit to give you someone with a godly character with whom you can share your heart and thoughts. He will give you someone who loves the Lord, and you will observe the Spirit of God shining through them. There is nothing wrong with getting some backup force from authentic people in the Lord. But remember, God is not going to tell anyone your business. When you share your concerns with people, they have to go to Christ for you. So go to Christ for yourself. We are humans, and we make mistakes. We must trust God and seek Him for everything, and He will keep us in perfect peace. God knows our future; He is *A Timeless God*. Even though we were *Born a Sinner, God Orchestrates Lives* during our *P.O.T. Experiences*. When we live in obedience to God, we will receive a *Neck-Turning Blessing*. We all have had *Spiritual Visitations* and a touch of the *Healing Power of God*. And remember that *Our Fight is Spiritual,* not natural with the enemy. We must *Keep Moving in Christ* by faith and remain *All-In* because we are more than conquers in Christ Jesus.